august 1993

New England
HOME FRONT
WORLD WAR II

Boston Evening Globe

(Reg. U. S. Pat. Off.)   Copyright, 1941, by the Globe Newspaper Co.

MONDAY, DEC. 8, 1941   VOL. CXL NO. 161   32 PAGES—TWO CENTS

WAR EXTRA!

Grim-Faced President Asks War

"DASTARDLY, UNPROVOKED ATTACK" — President Roosevelt shown addressing Congress at historical moment he charged Japan with aggression against United States.

CONGRESS VOTES WAR

SENATE: 82 to 0
HOUSE: 388 to 1

WASHINGTON, Dec. 8 (UP)—Congress today proclaimed existence of a state of war between the United States and the Japanese Empire 33 minutes after the dramatic moment when President Roosevelt stood before a joint session to pledge that we will triumph—"So help us, God."

Democracy was proving its right to a place in the sun with a split-second shiftover from peace to all-out war.

The Senate acted first, adopting the resolution by a unanimous rollcall vote of 82 to 0, within 21 minutes after the President had concluded his speech.

The House voted immediately afterward and by 1:13 p. m. a majority of the House had voted "aye."

The final House vote was announced as 388 to 1. The lone negative vote was cast by Representative Jeannette Rankin, Rep. of Montana, who also voted against entry in World War I.

The resolution now has to be signed by Speaker Sam Rayburn

and Vice President Henry A. Wallace before it is sent to the President at the White House. His signature will place the United States formally at war against the Japanese Empire, already an accomplished fact.

The resolutions were before both Houses within 15 minutes of the time Mr. Roosevelt ended his

seven-minute, 500-word extraordinary message

There was a half second of uncertainty in the House when Representative Jeannette Rankin, Rep., of Montana, objected to unanimous consent for immediate consideration of the war resolution.

Congress
Continued on Page 10

1500 DEAD IN HAWAII

WASHINGTON, Dec. 8 (AP)—The White House announced today that the Japanese attack on Hawaii had resulted in 3000 casualties, the capsizing of an old battleship, the destruction of a destroyer, damage to other vessels and destruction of a relatively large number of planes. It added that several Japanese planes and submarines had been accounted for.

An official White House statement, the first authentic government appraisal of the attack yesterday, said the casualties were expected to mount to about 3000, nearly half of them fatalities.

It was disclosed that active resistance was "still continu-

ing" against the Japanese attacking force in the vicinity of Hawaii. Reenforcements of planes are being rushed to the islands the White House said and repair work is under way on ships, planes and ground facilities

The White House said that

Wake and Midway Islands, in addition to the island of Guam and Hongkong. China, had been attacked, but that details were lacking.

Asked whether there was any official information why Japan was able to get inside the outer defenses of the Hawaiian group,

Presidential Secretary Stephen Early said it was the consensus of experts that probably all the attacking planes came from carriers which had moved forward during the night and sent their planes aloft. The attack came at dawn yesterday.

There was no identification of

the battleship which capsized beyond the statement that she was an old one. The ship turned over in Pearl Harbor, the Navy's giant Hawaiian base.

War
Continued on Page 10

Official Casualty List

By the Associated Press

Following is the list of members of United States armed forces killed in the war in the East, as disclosed by official advices to the next of kin:

First Lieut. Hans Christiansen, 21, Woodland, Calif., marine aviator, at Pearl Harbor.

Private George G. Leslie, 20, Arnold, Penn., Army Air Corps, at Hawaii.

Robert Niedzwiecki, 22, Grand Rapids, Mich., at Hawaii.

Second Lieut. Forge A. Whiteman, Sedalia, Mo., Air Corps, at Pearl Harbor.

Gordon Mitchell Hoisington, Kan., Air Corps, at Hawaii.

Private Donald Plant, 22, of Wausau, Wis., Air Corps, at Wheeler Field, Hawaii.

John Fletcher, 32, of Janesville, Wis., Air Corps, at Wheeler Field, Hawaii.

Lieut. James Derthick, 22, Ravenna, O., Army Air Corps, at Honolulu.

Private Dean W. Cebert of Galesburg, Ill., at Honolulu.

Sergt. James Guthrie, Republican Grove, Va., Air Corps Engineer, in Hawaii.

Sergt. George R. Schmersahl, 22, Roseland, N. J., Air Corps, at Hawaii.

Theo F. Byrd, 20, Tampa, Fla, private first class, Air Corps, at Wheeler Field, Hawaii, Sunday.

Text of F. D.'s Message

WASHINGTON, Dec. 8 (AP)—The text of President Roosevelt's war message to Congress follows:

To the Congress of the United States:

Yesterday, Dec. 7, 1941—a date which will live in infamy—the United States of America was suddenly and deliberately attacked by naval and air forces of the Empire of Japan.

The United States was at peace with that nation and, at the solicitation of Japan, was still in conversation with its government and its Emperor looking toward the maintenance of peace in the Pacific.

Indeed, one hour after Japanese air squadrons had commenced bombing in Oahu, the Japanese Ambassador to the United States and his colleague delivered to the Secretary of State a formal reply to a recent American message. While this reply stated that it seemed useless to continue the existing negotiations, it contained no threat or hint of war or armed attack.

It will be recorded that the distance of Hawaii from Japan makes it obvious that the attack was deliberately planned many days or even weeks ago. During the intervening time, the Japanese Government has deliberately sought to deceive the United States by false statements and expressions of hope for continued peace.

The attack yesterday on the Hawaiian Islands has caused severe damage to American naval and military forces. Very many American lives have been lost. In addition, American ships have

been reported torpedoed on the high seas between San Francisco and Honolulu.

Yesterday the Japanese Government also launched an attack against Malaya.

Last night Japanese forces attacked Hongkong.

Last night Japanese forces attacked Guam.

Last night Japanese forces attacked the Philippine Islands.

Last night the Japanese attacked Wake Island.

This morning the Japanese attacked Midway Island

F. D.

Continued on Page

Jap Planes Bombing Manila

NEW YORK, Dec. 8 (AP)—An N. B. C. reporter, broadcasting in the midst of an early Tuesday morning air attack on Manila said that "terrific damage" had been left by the Japanese attackers, including the apparent destruction of the gasoline supply at Nichols Airfield.

Don Bell, another N. B. C. man, standing above a bomb-

proof shelter said that the anti-aircraft fire, in progress for 15 minutes before he spoke, had quieted down.

At 2:32 p. m., E. S. T. (3:32 a. m., Tuesday, Manila time), Bell casually remarked that "Perhaps, ladies and gentlemen, you can hear the sound of those Japanese bombers again. Apparently the raid is not over yet."

Then Bell went on, saying that Corregidor, Army base guarding Manila, had been bombed but "nothing very serious happened."

MANILA, P. I., Dec. 8 (UP)—Press dispatches reported that

100 to 200 troops. 60 of them Americans, were killed tonight when Japanese warplanes raided Iba, on the west coast of the island of Luzon, north of the Olangapo naval base.

The Manila Tribune, a Filipino newspaper, said 200 troops were killed or injured at Iba and it said that 60 of the casualties were Americans. The American-owned Manila Daily Bulletin placed the casualties in the Iba raid at 100 killed or injured.

In addition to attacks on Iba and Clark Field, the Japanese

today bombed three other strategic points in the Philippines— Aparri at the northern tip of Luzon, Davao, great hemp center on the island of Mindano in the south and Palawan Island, westernmost of the larger Philippine Islands, on the Sulu Sea.

New England HOME FRONT

≣ WORLD WAR II ≣

TEXT BY ROBERT TAYLOR

YANKEE BOOKS

Jacket, text design and photo research by
AMY FISCHER, Camden, Maine

Additional photo research by
LINDA SPENCER and WENDY INGRAM

Typeset by TYPEWORKS, Belfast, Maine

Printed and bound in the United States

Frontispiece: Front page of *The Boston Globe* of December 8, 1941.
(Reprinted Courtesy of *The Boston Globe*.)

Library of Congress Cataloging-in-Publication Data

New England home front, WW II / by the staff of Yankee Books.
    p.   cm.
  ISBN 0-89909-333-7
  1. World War, 1939-1945 – New England – Pictorial works. 2. New
England – History – Pictorial works.   I. Yankee Books.
D769.85.N24N48 1991
940.53'74'0222 – dc20   91-30410
                             CIP

10 9 8 7 6 5 4 3 2 1

To those who remember the home front

CONTENTS

PREFACE

"December 7, 1941, is a date that will live in infamy," said President Franklin Delano Roosevelt in his historic speech before a joint session of Congress the day after the Japanese air force bombed Pearl Harbor. Congress responded by declaring war on Japan, and on December 11 Germany and Italy, faithful to their Axis ally, declared war on the United States.

At Pearl Harbor 2,403 American sailors, soldiers, marines, and civilians were killed and 1,178 more wounded. The U.S. lost 149 planes destroyed on the ground or in the water. The battleship *Arizona* was sunk beyond repair; the *Oklahoma* capsized; the *Tennessee*, *West Virginia*, and *California* were sunk, the *Nevada* run aground (to prevent sinking); two naval auxiliaries destroyed; three destroyers badly damaged. The Japanese force that flew the mission lost fewer than thirty men and planes and returned safely to their home base.

The Japanese attack on Pearl Harbor galvanized the American people as no other hostile act toward the United States has. The American war machine sprang into around-the-clock action and touched the lives of everyone, whether they lived in small towns, on farms, in cities. Men between the ages of 18 and 45 — from factory workers to college students — joined the armed forces and went off to fight. Over 15 million Americans served in the armed forces during the war: 10 million in the army, 4 million in the navy and coast guard, 600,000 in the marine corps. Approximately 216,000 women served as nurses and in the WAVES or WACS or as lady marines.

The folks at home, the older men, the women, and children of all ages, went to work. In New England, always a strong industrial area of the United States, folks responded by working twenty-four hours a day to build ships, air crafts, munitions, and every conceivable item needed to support the soldiers in the field.

Men and women living in Portland, Maine, built ships, in Springfield, Massachusetts, built munitions, in Hartford, Connecticut, built aircraft. Women learned auto mechanics at the Brighton Trade School in Massachusetts. In factories all across New England they did welding, riveting, and drove trucks and jeeps.

People of all ages recycled everything from flashlight batteries to metal tea pots. Children were enlisted to help in paper drives and in the collection of discarded rubber tires. Victory gardens were planted in front lawns on Main Street and on town commons in New England cities and towns. Folks organized U.S.O. dances, saw troops off to war, and held innumerable bond drives. They strung rolls of wire on beaches along the Atlantic coast, and older men patrolled the coast for Axis submarines. Every house hung blackout curtains, and everyone learned first aid — just in case. And all this was done for forty-five long months, from December 8, 1941, to that joyous day of August 14, 1945, when Japan, the last

Axis power still fighting in that summer of 1945, surrendered and the world knew peace.

To mark the fiftieth anniversary of Pearl Harbor, Yankee Books has created this photographic tribute to those New Englanders who stayed home and worked long, hard hours in their unprecedented support of American troops. Many of these photos have not been published since they first appeared in newspapers during the war. Some of the photos are from private collections and local historical societies. Collected together, they tell a story of untiring labor, commitment, and team work. To those folks who were part of the New England home front, we dedicate this book.

The Staff of Yankee Books

CREDITS AND ACKNOWLEDGMENTS

The staff of Yankee Books thanks the following organizations and individuals for permission to reproduce the photographs in this book:

Bangor Historical Society, Dr. Diane Vatne, Executive Director, Bangor, ME; Berkshire Athenaeum, Pittsfield Public Library, Pittsfield, MA, Ruth T. Degenhardt, Supervisor; The Bettman Archive, New York City; *The Boston Globe*, Boston, MA, Richard Gulla, Alfred S. Larkin, Jeanne Mulvaney; Boston National Historic Park, National Park Service, Brooke Childrey; *The Christian Science Monitor*, Boston, MA, R. Norman Matheny, Constance Dowcett, Jim Carlson; Connecticut Historical Society, Hartford, CT, Julie Kirkpatrick; Tony DeBonee, photographer, East Hartford, CT; Freeport Historical Society, Freeport, ME, Linda Sten; Hartford Public Library, Hartford, CT, Beverly A. Loughlin, Curator, Hartford Collection; Historical Society of Cheshire County, Keene, NH, Alan F. Rumrill; The Historical Society of the Town of Greenwich, Cos Cob, CT, Susan Richardson; Kelter-Malce Antiques, New York City, Cyril Nelson; Kennebunkport Historical Society, Kennebunkport, ME, Mary Messer, Patrice Tobin; Lynn Historical Society, Lynn, MA, Ken Turino; Maine Historical Society, Portland, ME, Nick Noyes, Steve Seames; Maine Maritime Museum, Bath, ME, Nathan Lipford; Maine State Archives, Augusta, ME, Jeff Brown; Massachusetts Historical Society, Boston, MA, Louis L. Tucker, Director, Chris Steele; Mount Holyoke College, South Hadley, MA, Anne C. Edmonds,

Patricia Albright, Sue Fliss, Elaine D. Trehub; National Park Service, Springfield Armory, Springfield, MA, Barbara Higgins Aubrey, Stan Skarzynski; Newport Historical Society, Newport, RI, Joan Youngken; North East Archives of Folklore and Oral History, University of Maine, Orono, ME, Kathy Corridan; *The Portland Press Herald*, Portland, ME, Sandy Schriver C.C. Church; The Schlesinger Library, Radcliffe College, Cambridge, MA, Marie-Hélène Gold; Smith College Archives, Smith College, Northampton, MA, Fred Chase, Margery N. Sly, Susan Boone; Society for the Preservation of New England Antiquities, Boston, MA, Lorna Condon, Arthur Griffin; South Portland Shipyard Society, South Portland, ME, Edward Langlois; Spring Point Museum, Portland, ME, William A. Bayreuther, Executive Director, Molly Horvath, Conservator, Michael Kazilionis, Joanne Kitch; Houston Photograph Collection, Vermont State Archives, Montpelier, VT, Cristie Carter, Gregory Sanford; L.L. McAllister Photograph Collection, Special Collections, University of Vermont, Burlington, VT, Reidun D. Nuquist, Reference Specialist; Roberta Wheaton and Fred Richards, Princeton, ME; Worcester Historical Museum, Joan Bedard Library, Ronald Bourgeson, Meredith Belding, Beverly Osborn; Aubrey Young, Camden, ME.

In addition the staff wishes to thank the following individuals and organizations for their help in locating material for this book: Isabelle Abbott, Union, ME; Ruth Aiken, Cushing, ME; Charlene S. Baer, Rhode Island Historical Society, Providence, RI; Edwin Battison, American Precision Museum, VT; The Bixby Library, Vergennes, VT; Barney Bloom, Vermont Historical Society; Catherine Bell, Houlton, ME; Boston Athenaeum, Boston, MA; Bostonian Society, Boston, MA, Philip Bergen; Sam Jones, Boynton-McKay Drug Store, Camden, ME; Richard Card, Boston, MA; Joe Carvello, Guy McClain, Cynthia Murphy, Connecticut Valley Historical Museum, Springfield, MA; Kenneth Cramer, Dartmouth College Archives, Hanover, NH, Culver Pictures, New York City; *Down East* magazine, Mike Chickering; Joel Eastman, History Department, University of Southern Maine, Portland, ME; Jim Fahey, Military Records, Natick, MA; Bruce Fraser, Mark Jones, Connecticut State Library, Hartford, CT; Wanda Harrington, Springfield Historical Society, Springfield, VT; Wayne Hockmeyer,

Northern Outdoors, The Forks, ME; Linda Honan, Higgins Armory Museum, Worcester, MA; Christine Lamar, Rhode Island State Archives, Providence, RI; Dan Lombardo, Jones Library, Amherst College, Amherst, MA; Laurie MacCallum, Connecticut Humanities Council, Middletown, CT; Errol Marden, Bangor, ME; Jeff Marshall, Bailey-Howell Library, University of Vermont, Burlington, VT; Anthony Nicolosi, Naval War College Museum, Newport, RI; Charles Norwood, *The Hartford Courant*, Hartford, CT; Esther O'Brien, Freeport, ME; Fred Pernell, Asst. Chief for Reference, Still Picture Branch, National Archives, Washington, D.C.; Karen Petersen, Rokeby Museum, Ferrisburg, VT; Mark Putnam, *The Star Herald*, Presque Isle, ME; Louise Rockwell, Cushing, ME; Ron Roussell, Maine Military Historical Society, Inc., Augusta, ME; Gary Sampson, Media Services Department, University New Hampshire, Durham, NH; Strawbery Banke, Portsmouth, NH, Marty McGannon; Jim and Tony Stamatelos, Cambridge, MA; Richard Trask, Danvers Archival Center, Danvers, MA; Mrs. Tricke, *The Houlton Pioneer Times*, Houlton, ME; Lorna Trowbridge, Yankee Publishing, Dublin, NH; Betsy Warner, Yarmouth Historical Society, Yarmouth, ME.

WAR DECLARED

During World War II, New England women, children, and men past draft age worked. They spent long hours in factories building ships, aircraft, and munitions. They grew their own food to insure a steady food supply, recycled every imaginable household item, bought bonds, and kept up the morale of troops overseas and their own morale. This Victory quilt is made-up of the "V" for victory sign and three dots and a dash, the Morse code symbol for the letter "V." During World War II the three dots and a dash became associated with the first four notes of the first movement of Beethoven's Fifth Symphony, frequently played on radio stations. *(Photograph courtesy Kelter-Malce Antiques, New York City)*

ON DECEMBER 7, 1941, A BRIGHT AND BRISK SUNDAY AFTER AN UNSEASONABLY WARM WEEK, READERS OF *THE BOSTON GLOBE* COULD TAKE REASSURANCE FROM A PROMINENTLY DISPLAYED FEATURE STORY, "GOLDEN OPPORTUNITY TO SMASH JAPAN," BY WILLIAM HARLAN HALE, DESCRIBED UNDER HIS BYLINE AS "AN AMERICAN HISTORIAN AND NAVAL Expert." "We could blow Japan's fleet out of the water — if we could get at it," Hale promised. "We would have Russia on our side, with sixty submarines ready to pounce from Vladivostok; a reinforced Netherlands Indies fleet would aid us from Surabaya; Japan would find herself overextended and half exhausted in her war with China; and we would have a dozen Allied bases to work from, the greatest being Singapore."

While New Englanders pondered Hale's militant prophecies or sought diversion in the sports pages, which featured Al Cannava's 105-yard touchdown run against the Salem Witches (Salem beat Medford 12–7 despite his heroics), somewhere in the vicinity a radio was playing. It was the golden age of broadcasting. Americans everywhere heard network programs like the popular Edgar Bergen and Charlie McCarthy comedy show, "The Inner Sanctum" mystery prefaced by a creaking door, and "One Man's Family" — all scheduled for Sunday evening. Sunday afternoons meant "The University of Chicago Round Table" or concerts by the New York Philharmonic: Artur Rubinstein would be the soloist that day on CBS, playing Brahms's Piano Concerto no. 2. At 2:31 P.M., however, the voice of announcer John Charles Daly broke through the clamor of the orchestra tuning up for the opening selection, Shostakovich's Symphony no. 1.: "We interrupt this program to bring you a special news bulletin. The Japanese have attacked Pearl Harbor, Hawaii, by air, President Roosevelt has just announced. The attack was also made on naval and military activities on the principal island of Oahu." He stumbled over the final word. Then everything continued as before, as if in those few seconds of time a way of life had not disappeared.

A few listeners retained their composure. Harvard Law School student Thomas Page was at the Agawam Hunt Club in Providence, where a friend was skeet shooting. He recalled: "I was sitting in a car listening to the New York Symphony when I heard it. For some odd reason, it did not really surprise me. The fact of Pearl Harbor, I think, surprised me, but I had decided about two weeks before that there was a very strong likelihood of war." But most people responded with incredulity. Journalist Marquis Childs thought, "Nothing will ever be the same again." Nor was it, for Childs or for 132 million fellow Americans.

The atmosphere in which New Englanders lived and worked in 1941 now seems as remote as Troy or Nineveh. A Kelvinator refrigerator sold for $133.10 ($5.00 down), a 1932 Ford roadster for $49.00, and a six-room colonial with four open fireplaces near Lake Winnipesaukee for $3500. A permanent wave at Gilchrist's

A thousand women joined the Army
at this recruitment ceremony in
Boston Garden. *(Courtesy
Massachusetts Historical Society)*

Naval recruits take the oath in
Boston's Symphony Hall as families
watch from balconies draped
with signal flags. *(Courtesy
Massachusetts Historical Society)*

department store cost sixty-five cents. As these prices indicate, the traumas of the Depression still lingered. Although the transition from an agricultural to an industrial society had taken place mostly during the 1920s, no section of the country remained more rural or isolated than many lantern-lit hamlets in Maine, New Hampshire, and Vermont. At the same time, regional differences were blending into contemporary life. The texture of 1941 included Ted Williams's batting average of .406, compiled when baseball at Fenway Park was played in daylight; movies for a nation of weekly movie-goers, from *Citizen Kane*, with Orson Welles, to *King's Row*, with Ann Sheridan, Robert Cummings, and Ronald Reagan; the popularity of photojournalism, *Life* magazine's mammoth circulation, and ads for products like the detergent Duz and Hires nickel root beer; comic strips like Milton Caniff's "Terry and the Pirates" and Al Capp's "L'il Abner"; big-band tunes like Glenn Miller's "Chattanooga Choo Choo," a recording that sold more than a million copies and prompted RCA Victor to spray a commemorative disc with gold paint; fashions like the snood and the calf-length dress with shoulder pads; and sentimental ballads like "The White Cliffs of Dover" and "This Love of Mine," with words credited to Frank Sinatra, who had yet to provoke hysteria among bobby-soxers at New York's Paramount Theatre.

In the week before Pearl Harbor, Boston's entertainment scene was dominated by the world-premiere engagement of the screen adaptation of J.P. Marquand's novel, *H.M. Pulham, Esq.*, Hollywood stars made personal appearances to promote the film, and Robert Young disclosed that Marquand had counseled him to "wear unpressed pants and a funny-looking tie," if he wanted to look like a Harvard student. Newspapers had a predilection for such fluff and seldom addressed complex issues of gender, race, and class. Women, barred from working in shipyards before the war, were consigned to domestic roles; the press for the most part ignored minorities; and in general, key social policies were established by white middle- or upper-class males. But all that would change in the next three-and-a-half years on the New England home front.

Leverett Saltonstall, the Republican governor of Massachusetts, driving to Chestnut Hill, heard the news over his car radio and immediately ordered out the entire State Guard to protect railroads and utilities. He was keenly aware of the submarine threat to New England's shores. The ongoing debate in the nation since the outbreak of war in Europe had pitted the internationalists, vulnerable to attack on either coast, against the isolationists, secure in the bastion of the Midwest. Their philosophic differences were instantly resolved by Pearl Harbor.

Greeting the chill dawn of December 8, forty-one men, headed by John R. Borts of Lawrence, waited in line for the opening of the recruiting office in the Boston Post Office, and before the day was over more than a thousand would enlist. Notwithstanding the rush of volunteers or the first peacetime draft, which had been in place a year, America was woefully unprepared to defend herself. Within the week, red-white-and-blue buttons ("Japan Started It/U.S. Will End It") adorned lapels, but patriotic euphoria coexisted with fear fueled by the unremittingly bleak news from the war zones. Rumors multiplied. The alarums of the first dark months of the war had, of course, some ludicrous aspects. Axis sympathizers were reported flashing messages to U-boats from the peak of Mt. Monadnock. *The Globe* published an article entitled "How to Tell a Chinese Apart from a Japanese," in which Harvard anthropologist

It was goodbye for the duration to the Golden Dome of the Massachusetts State House, which vanished like a setting sun beneath a layer of gunmetal-gray. *(Courtesy Massachusetts Historical Society)*

Ernest Hooton solemnly advised one to start by assessing the subject's height. Chinese-Americans wore buttons stating, "I Am a Chinese," and a prejudicial roundup of Japanese-Americans was underway. There were only one hundred Japanese-American citizens in all of New England, and two were seized in East Alburg, Vermont, working on a Central Vermont Railway freight train.

New England's immediate problem in December 1941 was preparation for the real possibility of air raids. Approximately ten thousand air raid wardens were recruited the first month in the Greater

Boston area, in teams composed mostly of middle-aged and older men and women, with a sizable sprinkling of high school students. A wardens' course was conducted by Boston police at the Mechanics Arts High School, and a thousand volunteers attended the Decem-16 session. Fears of attack were not groundless. Mayor Maurice Tobin predicted that Boston would be bombed; so did the Polish ambassador. The Massachusetts Committee on Public Safety and Office of Civilian Defense coordinated a uniform system of sirens and bells. Within days, fifteen thousand volunteer air raid wardens — one for every thirty-two square miles — went on twenty-four-hour alert. The blackout settled in for the duration, and three months after Pearl Harbor, the conspicuous gilt sparkle of the Massachusetts State House dome vanished beneath a coat of dull gray paint.

Scrap-metal drives (Saltonstall, who had crewed on a famous Harvard shell at Henley, donated his rowing machine to the war effort; the wrought-iron fence around Boston Common also went to war, never to return), victory gardens, and draft and rationing boards soon became fixtures on the home front. Sugar, butter, coffee, tires, and gasoline headed the ever-lengthening list of scarce items.

The war offered women unprecedented opportunities for employment; they were at first steered toward traditional roles in light manufacturing, clerical, and service areas, but as the demand mounted for weapons and equipment, training programs taught them the skills needed for heavy industry. Before Pearl Harbor, women comprised only one-quarter of America's labor force; then, in three years, some nineteen million women found jobs outside the home. Riveters, welders, and electricians, they were materially better off than they had ever been before. To be sure, at least a million others also performed necessary conventional tasks: they operated canteens, entertained servicemen, rolled bandages, donated blood, drove ambulances; but one of the enduring long-range effects of the war was the impact it made on the status of women. Filene's department store in Boston realized that women in skirts would be out of place on an assembly line and opened three Slack Bars.

The major shipyard and Navy towns — Bath, Portsmouth, Boston, Hingham, and Newport — worked round-the-clock shifts. So did the General Electric Company's River Works plant in Lynn, secretly assembling America's first jet engines. GE employed twenty-five thousand men and women. Because of the continuous work schedule, lifestyles altered dramatically. Theaters in Lynn and Boston showed films and stage shows in the morning. Bowling leagues competed in the morning as well. The Yankee Flyer diner just outside the GE plant was open twenty-four hours a day, seven days a week.

Relationships in this hectic setting seemed to burgeon, flower, and wilt like blossoms in stop-time photography. Every moment went into the war effort; no one seemed to have enough time for personal concerns; indeed, Marquand was to entitle his wartime novel *So Little Time*. The war, one was reminded, would be won at home, and diligent campaigns for bonds, wastepaper, and scrap testified to the nation's unity as vividly as the launching of a Liberty Ship. Bangor, Maine, shivered through north country winters without rubber boots for children or adults. Boston's kerosene storage tanks — filled with vital heating fuel — ran dry in February, and only a direct appeal to President Roosevelt freed a tanker and halted the

Young men take the oath
to defend the United States in
front of a compelling billboard.
(The Portland Press Herald)

evacuation of families in Chelsea, Somerville, and Quincy. Air raid sirens wailed over Provincetown — not to announce bombers, but to turn out the town onto the beaches, where the survivors of a torpedoed Allied merchantman needed assistance.

The home front inspired a community of purpose few would ever forget. Those touched by it would also remember its dark side: rent gouging, black marketeering, voluntary censorship. It was a period in New England life of mingled exhilaration, sadness, and upheaval, in which people were constantly coming together only to be torn apart. I was a 16-year-old student at Arlington High School on December 7, 1941; shortly after Pearl Harbor, Harvard University researchers came to the school seeking volunteers for a hush-hush program. We sat in darkened rooms where photographic images were projected onto a screen; the images, blurred and fragmented, could be brought together by a control handle and made to hover before a foreground "fence." Obviously, the project involved optics and sights, anti-aircraft perhaps, though to this day I have no idea what was happening; but when I recall the sweeping changes of those years (at the time of the Japanese surrender I was a twenty-year-old sailor in Borneo), the hours of manipulating broken images take on a symbolic quality. The photographic testament of the New England Home Front reveals in the pages that follow, the way things were, complete and whole.

INCREDIBLE
PRODUCTION FEATS

A model posing at the South
Portland shipyard in typical clothing
women wore while building the
ships: plaid shirt, work pants,
sturdy shoes and bandana. Plaid
clothing became fashionable during
the war. *(Northeast Archives of
Folklore and Oral History)*

WHEN WAR BROKE OUT, THE A.N. WETHERBEE COMPANY IN LYNDON, VERMONT, HAD BEEN MAKING TOY TOPS FOR MORE THAN A HALF CENTURY. WETHERBEE, IN FACT, HAD BECOME THE LARGEST TOY TOP MANUFACTURER IN THE WORLD, SPINNING OUT FIVE MILLION TOPS DURING A PROSPEROUS YEAR. IN 1942, FRANKLIN Roosevelt appointed Sears, Roebuck's vice-president, Donald M. Nelson, to be the nation's production czar, and one of the first things the newly formed War Production Board did was clamp down on the supply of metal and lumber. Wetherbee closed its doors.

Many firms, however, translated their line of merchandise into essential war products: Boston's Andrew Dutton Company, an awning and shade business, converted to making canvas for knapsacks and tents. The A.C. Gilbert Company of New Haven, Connecticut, discovered that the tiny motors that powered Gilbert Electric Trains could also be used for operating airborne navigational instruments. Because of the gargantuan size of plants like Pratt & Whitney in East Hartford, which manufactured airplane engines, or Willow Run outside Detroit, where every sixty-three

Timber cut entirely in Maine forests
became the source of
maritime barges. These lumberjacks
operated in 1942, before
the labor shortage was acute.
(Freeport Historical Society)

The Casco Shipbuilding Company
not only located and harvested the
lumber for barges but also milled it.
(Freeport Historical Society)

A handful of the 250 employees at the South Freeport, Maine, shipyard take a breather amid the ribs of a half-finished barge. The barges were 194 feet in length with a 34-foot beam.
(Freeport Historical Society)

A nonpropulsion cargo vessel contracted in 1943 by the U.S. Maritime Commission.
(Freeport Historical Society)

minutes, B-24 Liberator bombers flowed off a half-mile long assembly line, one tends to forget that component parts of the finished products came from smaller plants scattered throughout the country. Aircraft had protective paper wrappings from Maine, and in Pittsfield, Massachusetts, the General Electric Company worked on government contracts for crucial parts of what would become the atomic bomb. New England shipyards seethed around the clock and contributed to the avalanche resulting in $183 billion worth of war materials.

The machine shops of Holyoke, Massachusetts, soon became familiar to some Mt. Holyoke undergraduates. They shuttled to work in a program sponsored by the college and the National Youth Administration. *(Mount Holyoke College Library/Archives)*

Women filled roles once the prerogative of men. College students served in the timekeeper's cage as well as at the lathe.
(Mount Holyoke College Library/Archives)

On the job in a Holyoke machine shop where the snood was not only stylish but a practical accessory.
(Mount Holyoke College Library/Archives)

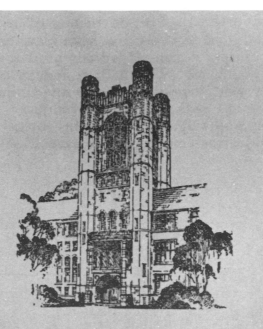

INDUSTRIAL WAR TRAINING PROGRAM

For Young Women

Jointly sponsored by:
National Youth Administration
Mount Holyoke College

at

Mount Holyoke College
South Hadley, Mass.
July 6 to August 28, 1942

The nation has begun to appreciate the full significance of industrial production in a war being fought by machines. So great are the labor demands that employment of women at mechanical war pursuits is no longer a matter of speculation. Hundreds of thousands of women are already at the lathes and drills which are producing guns and planes. Within these industries, the vital need today is for young women with traits of leadership and maturity who possess experience and training in machine shop work plus a background in the fundamentals of shop management and personnel techniques. Women with these qualifications are rapidly promoted to positions of authority and responsibility. This intensive 8-week training program* is designed to provide actual experience and training in machine shop work as well as a grounding in the elements of shop management and personnel work.

PROGRAM CONTENT

25 hours of machine shop experience per week on actual production work. (Under the supervision of the National Youth Administration.)

15 hours of machine shop theory per week. (Under the supervision of the Massachusetts Department of Education.)

6 hours of personnel and management training per week. (Under the supervision of Dr. Amy Hewes of Mount Holyoke College.)

LIVING FACILITIES

All members of the program will receive room and board in Mount Holyoke College campus dormitories and enjoy full use of all college recreational facilities. The dormitories will be operated on a cooperative basis, with all members participating in the serving of meals and general housekeeping arrangement.

FINANCIAL ARRANGEMENTS

All trainees will be paid thirty dollars ($30.00) per month for production work performed, of which twenty-two ($22.00) dollars per month will be deducted for subsistence costs. A charge of seventy-five cents ($.75) will be made for the use of recreational facilities over the 8-week period. There are no other fixed charges.

APPLICATIONS

1. Applicants must be between 17 - 24 years of age, inclusive.
2. Must have either suitable educational background or industrial experience.
3. Must be physically fit.
4. Must be out of school.
5. Must not be employed at time of application.
6. Must be an American Citizen.

This training program is, of necessity, limited to forty (40) trainees. The applicants will be selected so as to allow representation from both educational and industrial backgrounds.

Those interested should complete application blank on back cover and mail to either:

Dr. Amy Hewes
Department of Economics
    and Sociology
Mount Holyoke College
South Hadley, Mass.

OR

Division of Youth Personnel
National Youth Administration
10 Post Office Square
6th Floor
Boston, Mass.

*The final decision to offer this program is dependent upon the registration of a sufficient number of qualified persons.

Twenty-five hours of shop experience per week and a salary of $30 a month were among the incentives of Mt. Holyoke's industrial training program.
(Mount Holyoke College Library/Archives)

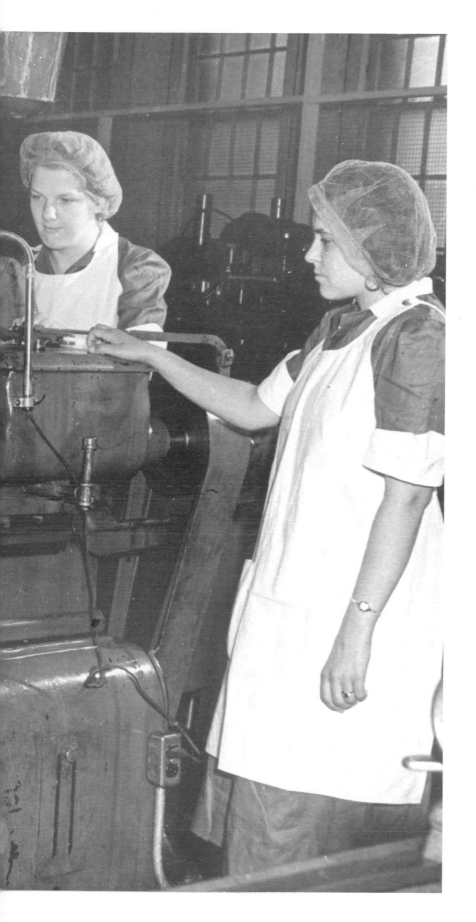

Training programs became a vital part of an accelerated production schedule. Here a group receives instruction from a senior mechanic. *(Mount Holyoke College Library/Archives)*

The Main Arsenal at the Springfield
Armory, built 1847-1850. The
famous Springfield Rifle was
developed here, as was the equally
famous M-1 Rifle, the U.S. infantry
weapon in World War II.
*(National Park Service, Springfield
Armory National Historic Site)*

John Garand invented the M-1 Rifle
while working at Springfield Armory.
*(National Park Service, Springfield
Armory National Historic Site)*

The interior barrel shop operations at the Springfield Armory. At the peak of production in 1943, the work force at the Armory numbered nearly fourteen thousand. The scale and size of operations like this was repeated in plants across the nation. *(National Park Service, Springfield Armory National Historic Site)*

Apprentice training at Springfield
Armory. The female welder became
a home-front fixture. Women
represented 45 percent of the work
force during World War II, filling in
at every level in what had been
considered strictly a male preserve.
*(National Park Service, Springfield
Armory National Historic Site)*

At the age of 63, Temofey
Stelmakoff (right) learns the trade
of a Springfield Armory machinist.
Age was no bar on the swing shift.
*(National Park Service, Springfield
Armory National Historic Site)*

Charles H. Hills grinding rifle
barrels at Springfield Armory.
During World War II many blacks
and other minorities found
employment in skilled fields for the
first time. *(National Park Service,
Springfield Armory National
Historic Site)*

A woman worker at a small press in
the Hardings fabrication plant of
the Bath Iron Works. *(Maine
Maritime Museum)*

In 1943, the launching of a ship—in this case the destroyer *Ingersoll*—attracted a throng as large as any at a movie premiere. *(Maine Maritime Museum)*

Sliding through the flakes of a chill February day in 1943 at the Bath Iron Works, the destroyer *Abbott* (DD-629) joins the Atlantic fleet. *(Maine Maritime Museum)*

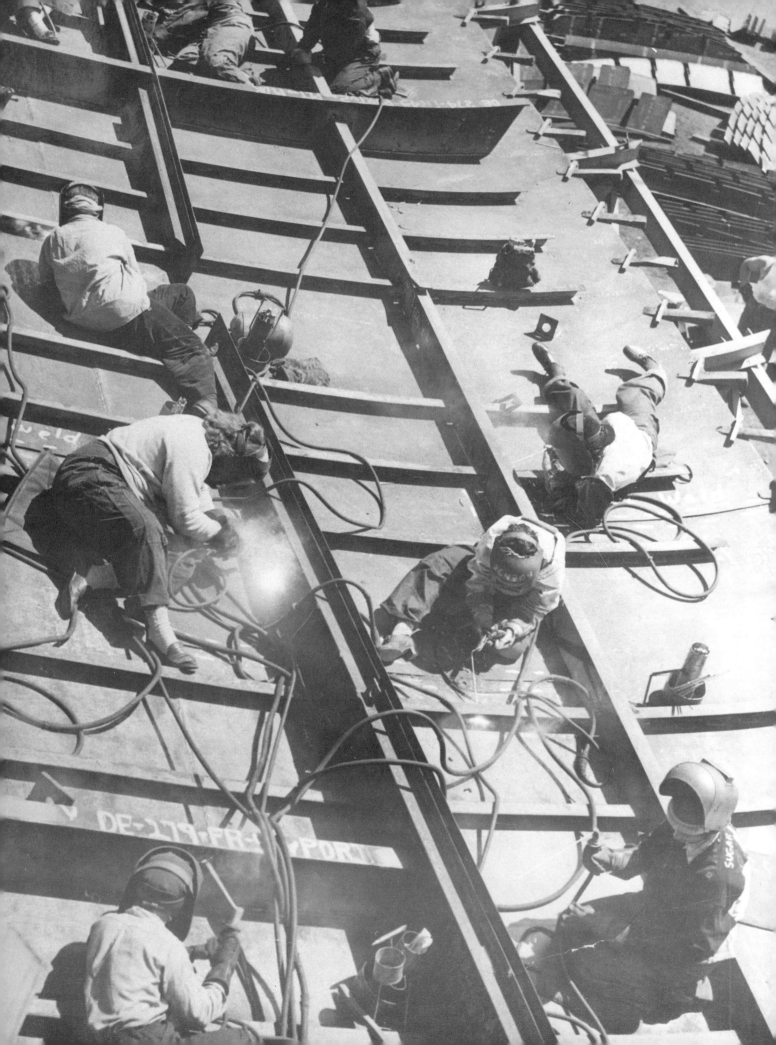

Women welders at Charlestown
Navy Yard as they fit out a destroyer
escort for sea make a pattern of
dramatic lights and shadows.
(Courtesy of National Park Service)

Round-the-clock shifts found
women working with heavy metal
at Charlestown Navy Yard.
(Courtesy of National Park Service)

Like pieces of an interlocking jigsaw
puzzle, giant dielock chains—
used in anchors and in railroads—
surround workers on flatbed cars
at Charlestown Navy Yard.
(*Courtesy of National Park Service*)

Each massive link of a dielock chain
was individually hammered out.
(Courtesy of National Park Service)

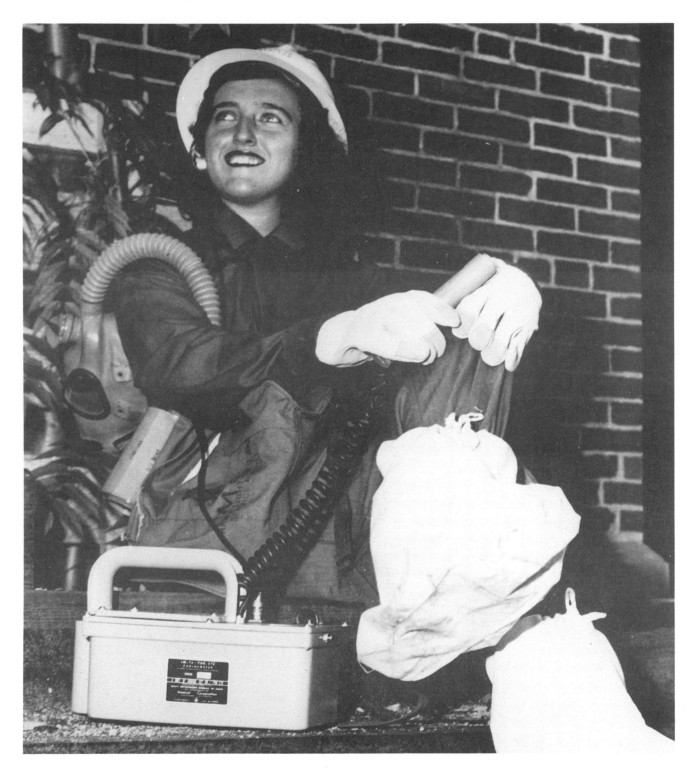

New technologies accompanied
the war effort. This woman
at Charlestown Navy Yard used
a Geiger counter in her job.
(Courtesy of National Park Service)

Precision skills were necessary in the core room of the Saco-Lowell Foundry in Biddeford, Maine, early in 1943. *(Northeast Archives of Folklore and Oral History)*

Maine Governor Sumner Sewall
with Eleanor Roosevelt at the
Camden Shipbuilding Company's
launching of the seagoing barge,
Pine Tree, February 8, 1943.
(Maine Maritime Museum)

Ocean rescue tug ATR 77, under
construction at the Camden
Shipbuilding Company in 1944.
(Maine Maritime Museum)

A 200-foot seagoing barge is
launched after dark at the Camden
Shipbuilding Company.
(Maine Maritime Museum)

A Christmas mass at the New
England Shipbuilding Corporation
yard. Working clothes are the norm.
(Maine Maritime Museum)

In the depths of a Maine winter, the miracle of continuous production went on. South Portland's New England Shipbuilding Corporation had three hulls underway.
(Maine Maritime Museum)

These five photographs illustrate
the sequence of modular-built
Liberty Ship Construction during
1942-43.
(Spring Point Museum)

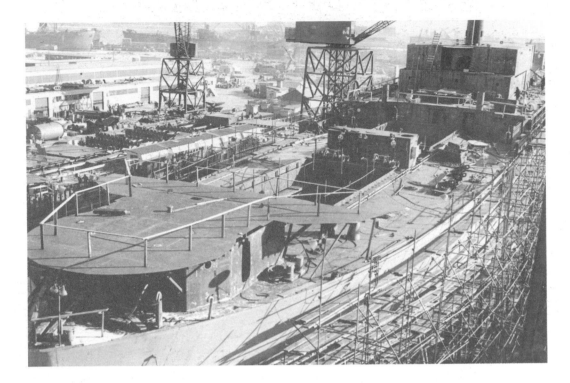

During peak production, over 30,000 people were employed at the two South Portland shipyards. Three shifts worked around the clock, seven days a week. Over 265 Liberty Ships were constructed, each taking an average of fifty-two days to build. Thirty British "Ocean" ships were completed in twenty-three months. *(Spring Point Museum)*

The Liberty Ship
Length: 441'-6"
Beam: 57'

The resolution on the features of this hard-hatted model caused her shipyard picture to be widely distributed as a symbol of women on the home front. *(Spring Point Museum)*

Aerial view of the launching of the
Liberty Ship *Thomas Hooker*,
July 18, 1942, in South Portland.
(Maine Maritime Museum)

Brotherhood and interfaith dinners were a prominent part of morale-boosting in the manufacturing sector. *(Bangor Historical Society)*

Production line at the Firestone
plant in Fall River, attaching steel
snaps to assault gas masks. Later
the masks were carried by troops
during the Normandy invasion.
(The Bettmann Archive)

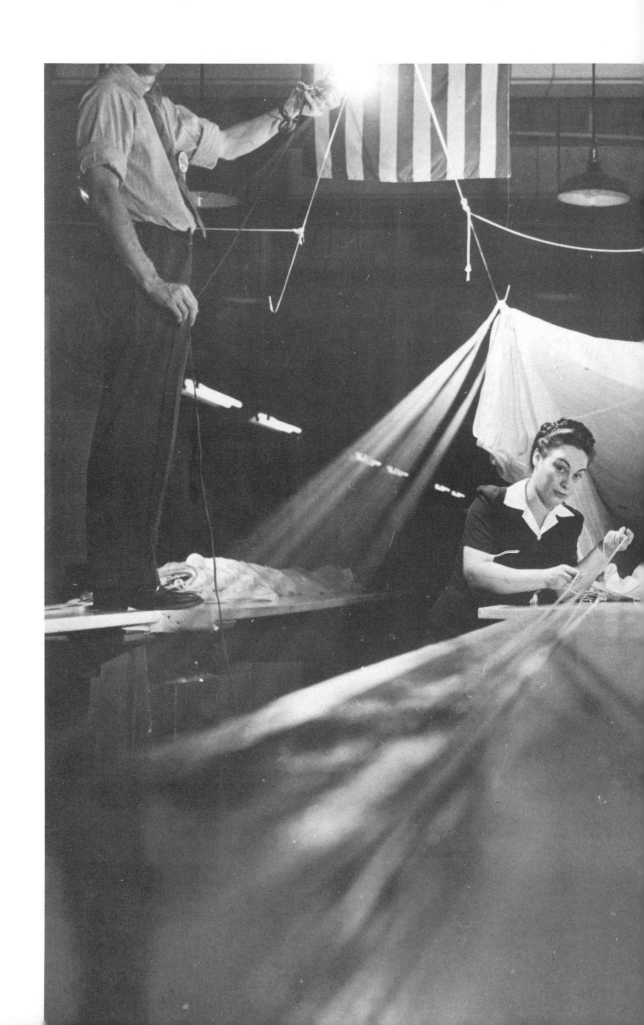

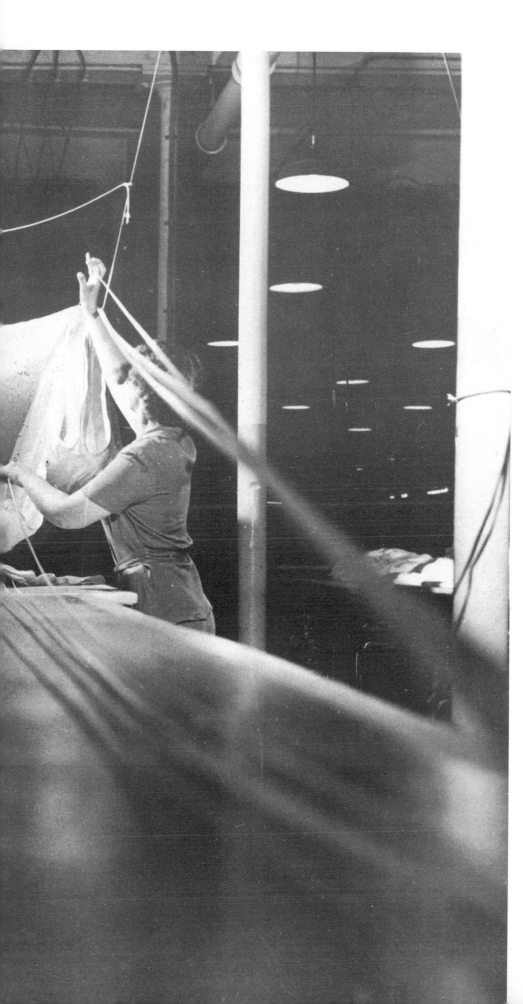

At the Pioneer Parachute Company, Inc., Manchester, Connecticut, suspension lines are carefully checked to determine that each is in its correct position in the canopy. *(The Schlesinger Library, Radcliffe College)*

Adeline Gray, nationally known parachutist, prepares to make the first actual live jump with a nylon parachute from the Pioneer Parachute Company, Manchester, Connecticut. *(The Schlesinger Library, Radcliffe College)*

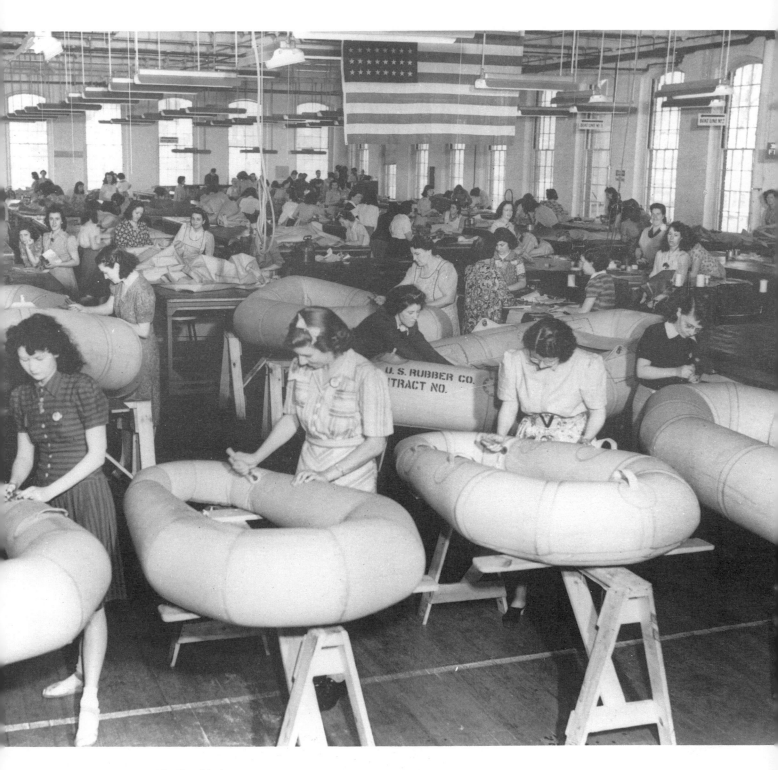

Mass production of inflatable boats
that helped save lives of
flyers shot down over water.
(The Bettman Archive)

In foreground, women apply seats
and accessories to rubber rafts
while others apply a coat of rubber
paint to the bottom of a boat.
*(The Schlesinger Library,
Radcliffe College)*

Workers at a Rhode Island naval
torpedo station mesh their
specialties together as
though choreographed. *(Newport
Historical Society)*

The deadly intricacies of a torpedo—fuses, circuitry, and coils— presented no obstacle to these women workers. *(Newport Historical Society)*

Assembling the components of a torpedo demanded precision measurement. *(Newport Historical Society)*

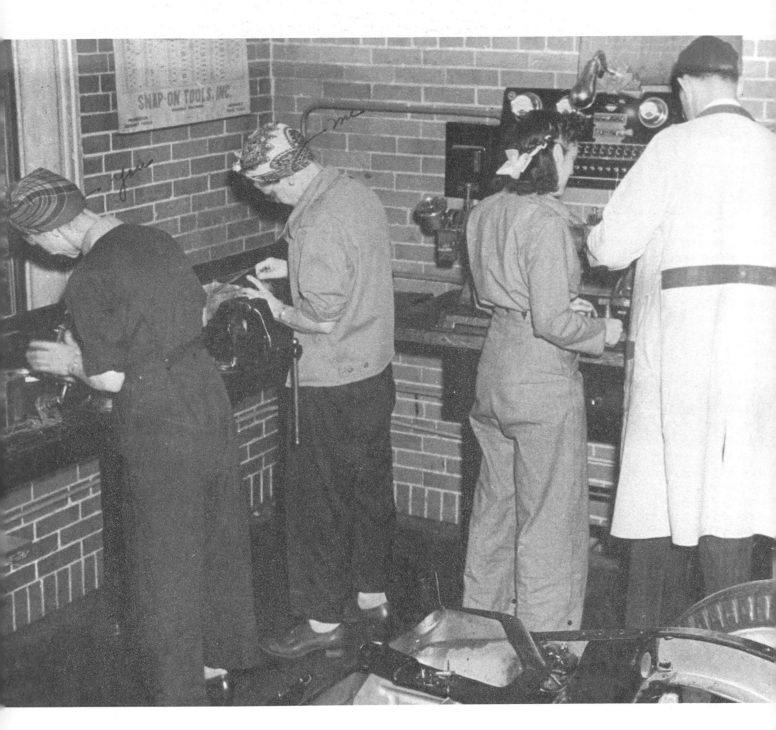

Three women and their instructor at
the benches of a repair shop in the
Brighton Trade School, Brighton,
Massachusetts, that trained women
during the war. *(Northeast Archives
of Folklore and Oral History)*

The war brought about social
revolution that cut across gender,
race, and class. Here ten women
learn mechanics from their shop
instructor at Brighton Trade School.
*(Northeast Archives of Folklore
and Oral History)*

Women students at Brighton Trade
School learning how to jack up
a truck and change a jumbo tire.
*(Northeast Archives of Folklore
and Oral History)*

Women mastered mechanics. Here
women at the Brighton Trade
School work on a vehicle.
*(Northeast Archives of Folklore
and Oral History)*

The Army and Navy awarded "E" for Excellence to firms that turned out quality work like the Boston Machine Works Company in Lynn. The size of the company was no factor. *(Lynn Historical Society)*

In Malden, Massachusetts, the
National Company received the
honorable Navy "E" for Excellence.
*(Courtesy of Massachusetts
Historical Society)*

THE GREAT
SCAVENGER HUNT

In Arlington, Massachusetts, Mrs.
Russell T. Hamlet, Chairman of the
Women's Division of the Public
Safety Committee, festooned herself
with aluminum pots and pans and
collected "defense metal" from
Mrs. James K. McKeown.
(The Boston Globe)

NEW ENGLAND AND THE NATION WENT ON ONE OF THE GREATEST SCAVENGER HUNTS IN HISTORY WHEN PRODUCTS FROM PAPER TO TIN CANS VANISHED FROM CONSUMER VIEW.

IN 1775, GENERAL HENRY KNOX HAD HAULED BRITISH CANNON CAPTURED FROM FORT TICONDEROGA TO RELIEVE THE SEIGE OF BOSTON, and a reenactment of this event inspired communities along the route to donate cannon and other weapons from town-hall lawns and village commons. Eventually these reached Boston, where they were converted into more contemporary ordnance. School children turned out to be the most zealous collectors of old paper, rags, rubber objects, and assorted junk. They even collected milkweed pods, which were used to stuff life jackets.

Every day of the war found salvage drives going on somewhere. Farmers recycled and patched burlap grain sacks (burlap, from India, had almost disappeared), vests no longer came with men's suits, nor did trouser cuffs. Flashlight batteries were all but unobtainable. Malden, Massachusetts, had a weekly collection of fats and greases, which yielded glycerines for high explosives. Kids in Providence, Rhode Island, went from door to door asking residents to contribute aluminum for scrap. Recycling was a way of life. Paper had gone the way of the trouser cuff, because the lumber-jacks of Maine and the Pacific Northwest could not be replaced, even by prisoners of war (permitted under the Geneva Convention). Toward the end of the war, though, an ingenious publisher in Cambridge attempted to start a general-interest magazine that would be printed on the wrappings of soap. He obtained the soap wrappers but, alas, not the financial backing he needed.

A troop of Portland Boy Scouts turning in tires during a rubber salvage drive.
(The Portland Press Herald)

Patriotic grime. These mudlarks, members of the Boys Club of Greenwich, Connecticut, salvaged tires in 1942 from Horseneck Creek. *(Historical Society of the Town of Greenwich)*

Billboards in Hartford took on a patriotic look, but recycling still mingled old-fashioned sex appeal and salesmanship. *(Tony DeBonee)*

At a Mobilgas station in Portland a
driver hands over his ration card,
still something of novelty in 1942.
(The Portland Press Herald)

INSTRUCTIONS

1. This is your gasoline ration card for the vehicle or at described hereon. This card must last at least through June 30, 1942, in the rationed area. This card must be presented to your dealer for cancelation of one or more units each time you purchase gasoline.

2. This card can be used only for gasoline delivered i the fuel tank of the vehicle described hereon; or, if a b for gasoline to be used therein.

3. The value of the unit may be changed from time to on announcement by the Office of Price Administration.

4. Your local rationing board alone can make adjustmer or issue a different card.

U. S. GOVERNMENT PRINTING OFFICE : 1942—O-455906

Stamps were required for extra gas. Although the penalties for counterfeiting were stiff, black markets prospered. *(The Christian Science Monitor, R. Norman Matheny photo)*

Gas stations had to answer to rationing boards for the proper handling of cards like this one. *(The Christian Science Monitor, R. Norman Matheny photo)*

The bureaucratic complications
of price control are evident in the
dotted lines of a ration book.
(The Christian Science Monitor,
R. Norman Matheny photo)

The cover for the war ration books that shoppers had to produce at the checkout counter. *(The Christian Science Monitor, R. Norman Matheny photo)*

Children bring Edison and Vocalion
records to a Portland movie theater
for free admission. *(The Portland
Press Herald)*

A JOB
ONLY
A WOMAN
CAN DO !

Approved by Salvage Division,
War Production Board

The War Production Board appealed
directly to women to recycle
everything—including waste fats.
*(Northeast Archives of Folklore
and Oral History)*

In 1942 a Portland meat counter
could advertise itself as an Official
Fat Collecting Station. And sirloin
was forty-five cents a pound.
(The Portland Press Herald)

Maine schoolboys collecting lard, a World War II ritual. *(Bangor Historical Society)*

The tempo of scrap collecting picked up as the war accelerated. Here a Vermont team fills a container railroad car in the spring of 1945. *(L.L. McAllister Photograph Collection, Special Collections, University of Vermont)*

In 1942, Governor William Wills of
Vermont contributes his number 1
license plate to the war effort.
*(Houston Photograph Collection,
Vermont State Archives)*

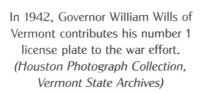

Governor Saltonstall (hard hat) was on hand as the Atlantic Avenue stop on the Boston El was dismantled for scrap in March 1942. *(Courtesy Massachusetts Historical Society)*

A salvage campaign poster issued
by the War Production Board.
Among other items, the board
urged turning in old batteries,
golf clubs, and broiler drippings.
(The Bettmann Archive)

In order to save gas, two eras of transportation overlap in a Hartford milk truck. *(Tony DeBonee)*

Eben O. Kimball of Lenox ran this shuttle between Lenox and the Berkshire Music Tent at Tanglewood, Massachusetts. Not much gas was saved (note the cars in the background) but everyone appears festive. *(Berkshire Athenaeum)*

The recycled paper drive was in full
swing when these trucks unloaded
onto Canadian Pacific boxcars at
Keene, New Hampshire, in 1944.
*(Historical Society of Cheshire
County, Keene, New Hampshire)*

In 1943, Pittsfield's school children aided the salvage committee in a drive to collect obsolete business forms. *(Berkshire Athenaeum)*

Scouts from Pittsfield's Troop No. 1
flank an elevated roadster as an
honor guard on the eve of Salvage
Sunday. *(Berkshire Athenaeum)*

For Pittsfield high school students an overflowing paper collection truck was their contribution to the war effort. *(Berkshire Athenaeum)*

Crates, corrugated boxes, and
kids—a potent combination
in recycling circa 1943 in Pittsfield.
(Berkshire Athenaeum)

In a scene reminiscent of an "Our Gang" film comedy, Bobby Ford, Malcolm Keeler, Paul Mathews, and Bobby's unidentified pooch contribute to Pittsfield's scrap drive. *(Berkshire Athenaeum)*

YOU AND YOUR FUEL OIL RATION

*The Why and How of Fuel Oil Rationing
and What To Do About It!*

How to stretch home fuel oil rations
through a New England winter
was the subject of frequent
conversation and official manuals.
(Lynn Historical Society)

THE
VICTORY FARMERS

They were called "Tractorette
Trainees," a diminutive that sounds
strange today, but Smith College
students learned offbeat tasks,
such as growing corn for ensilage.
(Smith College Archives)

"**W**E HAD GUARANTEED TO SUPPLY FOURTEEN ACRES OF CARROTS, BEETS, AND BEANS TO THE CANADIAN GOVERNMENT," AMY BESS MILLER, DIRECTOR OF THE SHAKER VILLAGE IN HANCOCK, MASSACHUSETTS, TOLD SOCIAL HISTORIAN ROY HOOPES. "THEY WERE GOING to send flatcars for them and can them there. The vegetables were just in marvelous shape, all ready to be called for on the first day of September — and we had a killing frost on August 26! The beans were ruined and the beet tops and carrot tops." Next came a letter from the Canadians stating they couldn't spare the flatcars. What to do with the surviving produce? Home freezing was in its infancy. Eventually, the crop was distributed among charitable agencies, but food on the New England home front could be a matter of surpluses as well as shortages.

Secretary of Agriculture Claude R. Wickard, conceived the notion of the Victory Garden shortly after Pearl Harbor, and by 1943 there were 20.5 million backyard gardens supplying one-third of the vegetables consumed in the United States. They sprouted in such unlikely sites as the middle of Boston's Copley Square and a park in Portland, Maine. War Rationing Book Number One, which appeared in March 1942, in a mammoth press run of 190 million copies, dealt with shortages of sugar and coffee (comedian Fred Allen sent the Roosevelts a single coffee bean for Christmas). A year later, soups, canned juices, meat, fish, and dairy products joined the list of rationed food. Shopping became a bewildering experience. Consumer "point values" were assigned, and each month everyone received fresh ration stamps and revised figures for either the blue coupon book (canned goods) or the red (meat, fish, and other commodities).

New Englanders, it was said, had forgotten what white or dark meat looked like; and the maintenance of farming equipment was as difficult as the dispersal of food. But more than a million 4-H members generated three million bushels of vegetables and fourteen million jars of preserves. The impact of the Victory Gardens may have been mostly psychological, since farms were already producing enough to sustain nutritional levels; nevertheless, in the long run, the gardens altered eating habits so that Americans were probably healthier in World War II than they had ever been before.

Governor Saltonstall looks over the Victory Garden on Boston Common. *(Courtesy Massachusetts Historical Society)*

Governor Saltonstall presents
Victory Garden awards to the young
farmers in charge of the harvesting
of Boston Common. *(Courtesy
Massachusetts Historical Society)*

Massachusetts Park Commissioner
William Long plows up a four-acre
plot of Boston's Franklin Park.
*(Photograph by Arthur Griffin,
courtesy of the Society for the
Preservation of New England
Antiquities)*

The thriving Victory Garden behind
Smith College's Neilson Library.
(Smith College Archives)

Mrs. Hazel Wills, wife of the
governor of Vermont, William Wills
(1941-45), started her own Victory
Garden. *(Houston Photograph
Collection, Vermont State Archives)*

A pig trough was more than
an abstraction to Smith College
undergraduates in 1943.
(Smith College Archives)

Young women in the Volunteer Land
Corps at Smith College learn to
come to grips with the livestock,
1943. *(Smith College Archives)*

"Victory calves," a thousand registered Jersey bulls, were donated to farmers as an encouragement to production. This one went to Sibley Farms in Spencer, Massachusetts. *(Courtesy Massachusetts Historical Society)*

Picking potatoes with the Women's Land Army of Maine when farm labor was in short supply. *(Northeast Archives of Folklore and Oral History)*

The potato harvest at Fort Fairfield,
Maine, took place in 1945
with fewer workers in the field.
(Maine State Archives)

Women were the predominant
potato pickers in the potato fields
of Aroostook County, Maine.
(Maine State Archives)

Food production was vital
during the war. Here barrels
of Maine potatoes from
Fort Fairfield are trucked away.
(Maine State Archives)

Keene, New Hampshire, Teachers College students who became "farmerettes." They picked potatoes one day a week for the five-week season, 1943. *(Historical Society of Cheshire County)*

The German prisoner-of-war camp
in Washington County, Maine,
remains one of the better-kept
secrets of the war. By day the
prisoners worked in the blueberry
fields and returned to a former
Conservation Corps Camp at night.
(Fred Richards)

Mt. Holyoke students breaking topsoil for the college's Victory Garden at South Hadley, Massachusetts, during the early spring of 1943. *(Mount Holyoke College Library/Archives)*

First Lady of the State of Maine,
Helen Sewall, and the Lubec unit of
the Women's Emergency Farm
Service in 1944. *(Northeast Archives
of Folklore and Oral History)*

April 1944 promotional pamphlet for the Women's Emergency Farm Service of Maine, also known as the Women's Land Army. *(Northeast Archives of Folklore and Oral History)*

THE WEFS OF

A division of the WOMEN'S LAND ARMY in the State of Maine for women living away from home while serving in the Agricultural Field of War Activities.

The workers are placed on individual Farms and in Camps. Great care is taken in the placement and supervision of women who enlist in this service.

REQUIREMENTS FOR ENROLLMENT.—Two character references and a health certificate for girls and women over eighteen years of age who will serve for at least two weeks.

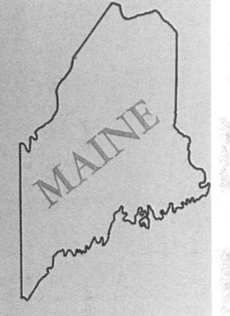

MAINE

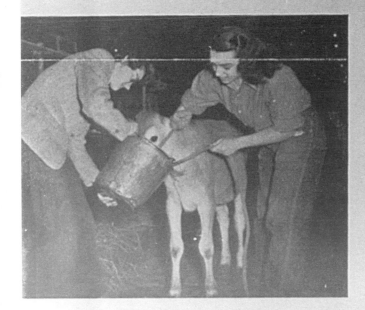

OPPORTUNITIES

Dairy Farming

Poultry Farming

Truck Gardening

Orchard Work

Berry Picking

Harvesting

WE NEED workers the year round for dairy and poultry farming.

Hands-on experience with
the plow and harrow. Like other
women's colleges, Mount Holyoke
joined traditional liberal arts
courses with crash war programs.
*(Mount Holyoke College
Library/Archives)*

A lull in the plowing of the
Mount Holyoke College Victory
Garden. Note the turned-up jeans
and bobby sox—campus chic in
1943. *(Mount Holyoke College
Library/Archives)*

Trimming and tying beets in
Northampton, 1943.
(Smith College Archives)

It was common during the war that folks stacked their cellars with home preserves, lessening their need for fresh groceries.
(Northeast Archives of Folklore and Oral History)

Storing pickles and peppers
and jams in the crowded cellar
shelves of Portland.
(The Portland Press Herald)

Mrs. Margurite Bartlett of East Bethel, Maine, inspects jars of chicken in her kitchen in 1942. *(Northeast Archives of Folklore and Oral History)*

THE MORALE BOOSTERS

Departures on train platforms like
this one from Portland, Maine, were
an everyday occurrence. *(Maine
Historical Society)*

A

HOT DOG AND ROOT BEER EMPORIUM ON BOSTON'S SCOLLAY SQUARE, THE CITY'S TENDERLOIN, DISPLAYED A SATIRIC MURAL, "WHAT SAILORS DO ON LIBERTY." ACCORDING TO THIS REPRESENTATION, SAILORS SNIFFED FLOWERS, LICKED ICE CREAM CONES, AND COMPORTED THEMSELVES WITH THE STARCHY DECORUM OF FLOORWALKERS in expensive department stores. In fact, homesick soldiers and sailors from small towns in Nebraska and Tennessee wandered through the streets of Worcester, Pawtucket, and Portsmouth like confused tourists. The answer to their ennui was the volunteer program.

The U.S.O., The United Service Organizations, was formed late in 1941 after meetings between President Roosevelt, Paul V. McNutt, then head of the Federal Security Agency, and military leaders. Out of these meetings evolved the U.S.O. network of three thousand U.S.O. clubs and canteens, where servicemen met, chatted, and danced with volunteer hostesses; every New England city had its U.S.O. center, and frequently Hollywood or sports celebrities on war bond or blood donation drives would entertain there.

The American Red Cross had elected to stay out of the U.S.O., preferring to present its own volunteer programs. These included the operation of mobile canteens and blood donor stations, workshops for rolling bandages, and courses in survival. In Keene, New Hampshire, the Red Cross sponsored antisubmarine drills, and in Rhode Island, older women participated in round-the-clock skywatching.

Not every unpaid volunteer program involved direct troop support. Naturally, U.S.O. relationships blossomed as well, and these

A Worcester trolley becomes a rolling billboard for the war effort, complete with stars and eaglets. *(Worcester Historical Museum)*

acquired intensity because no one knew how long they would last. The 1941 marriage rate was the highest ever recorded in the United States; the 1945 divorce rate also set a record. On the lighter side, women served as newsboys when the *Boston Record-American* returned to horse-drawn delivery. And though she wasn't a volunteer, a Newport dowager helped relieve the tensions of wartime as she sputtered around town in a beach chair propelled by a motorcycle engine.

On September, 19, 1942, Dorothy Lamour, sarong siren of the Bob Hope–Bing Crosby "Road" films, rides up Main Street, Keene, New Hampshire, promoting War Bonds. *(Historical Society of Cheshire County, Keene, New Hampshire)*

There was a massive Central Square
turnout for the Keene, New
Hampshire, War Bond drive
featuring Dorothy Lamour.
*(Historical Society of Cheshire
County, Keene, New Hampshire)*

Signs all over the main post office
in Boston urge customers to
buy bonds. *(Photograph by Arthur
Griffin, courtesy of the Society
for the Preservation of New England
Antiquities)*

Results from a Massachusetts 1942 Thanksgiving War Fund drive (note the Pilgrim hat) are posted in the state capitol building. *(Photograph by Arthur Griffin, courtesy of the Society for the Preservation of New England Antiquities)*

War bonds were sold in department
stores and plugged enthusiastically
by Hartford businesses.
(Tony DeBonee)

Throughout the war, the backdrop of the Massachusetts State House adorned fund-raising events, such as the United War Fund parade in October 1944. *(Courtesy Massachusetts Historical Society)*

Bay State Governor Leverett
Saltonstall welcomes comedienne
Gracie Allen and her husband
George Burns during their war bond
appearances. *(Courtesy
Massachusetts Historical Society)*

Military hardware like this
submarine in Hartford attracted
crowds at bond rallies.
(Tony DeBonee)

A tank rolls through downtown
Hartford during a parade
of weaponry. *(Tony DeBonee)*

WAVE petty officers in a Bangor
recruiting office. The women's
branch of the Navy observed many
of the same service traditions as the
men. *(Bangor Historical Society)*

The Women's Army Corps recruiting booth on Boston Common was later joined by its Navy or WAVES counterpart. In the booth: Mayor Maurice Tobin and Governor Saltonstall. *(Courtesy Massachusetts Historical Society)*

Entrance to the Buddies' Club on
Boston Common. The serviceman's
recreation center, still in its early
stages, has just been landscaped.
(Massachusetts Historical Society)

Sailors on shore leave flock to the
U.S.O. in South Boston.
*(Photograph by Arthur Griffin,
courtesy of the Society for the
Preservation of New England
Antiquities)*

Stewart's Rhythm band entertains
the troops at the U.S.O. in Hartford,
Connecticut. *(Hartford Collection,
Hartford Public Library)*

Actor Raymond Massey bantering
with service personnel at
the U.S.O. Snack Bar in Boston.
(The Bettmann Archive)

Grey Ladies, Mrs. Oliver and
Mrs. Wright, show off their
uniforms. A Red Cross volunteer
association, the Grey Ladies worked
in armed services hospitals.
*(Northeast Archives of Folklore
and Oral History)*

Smith College students fold
Red Cross bandages.
(Smith College Archives)

Students from Regis College,
Weston, Massachusetts, line up to
give blood. *(Photograph by Arthur
Griffin, courtesy of the Society
for the Preservation of
New England Antiquities)*

The ubiquitous Massachusetts
Governor, Leverett Saltonstall,
joins Red Cross blood donors in
a glass of orange juice, 1942.
*(Courtesy of Massachusetts
Historical Society)*

The Massachusetts Women's Defense Corps was founded by Natalie Hays Hammond before World War II but continued its operations as part of the civilian war effort. *(Photograph by Ansel Adams, MWDC, courtesy The Schlesinger Library, Radcliffe College)*

Movies were the great escape for
millions from the tensions and
uncertainties of the war years.
(Tony DeBonee)

The radio was one of the sources
for news from the war front.
*(Courtesy of Spring Point Museum,
Michael Kazilionis)*

Mannequins in a Bangor, Maine,
store window recruit civil defense
plane spotters as well as
direct enlistments. *(Bangor
Historical Society)*

Rosanna Thorndike, chairman
of the Boston Food Fund Committee
of the American Friends of France,
accepts canned food from children
of the North Bennet Street
Industrial School for refugee
children in France. *(The Schlesinger
Library, Radcliffe College)*

Grant's Department Store in Bangor
sold novelty turbans ($1.33), and
next to the turbans women
displayed photos of their men at
war and sold war bonds. *(Bangor
Historical Society)*

Bake sale in Bangor on behalf of
bonds. Cupcakes sold for five cents
a piece; whole cakes sold for
seventy-five cents. *(Bangor
Historical Society)*

THE HOME GUARD

This snug air raid shelter wasn't
constructed during the London Blitz;
it was made from concrete culvert
pipe for employees of the Vought-
Sikorsky aircraft factory in Stratford,
Connecticut. *(UPI/Bettman)*

WHILE JAPANESE BOMBS FELL ON PEARL HAR-
BOR, NEWTON, MASSACHUSETTS, COINCIDEN-
TALLY, WAS STAGING AN AIR RAID REHEARSAL.
THE OFFICE OF CIVILIAN DEFENSE UNDER NEW
YORK'S MAYOR FIORELLO LaGUARDIA HAD BEEN OPERATIVE FOR A
YEAR — SUDDENLY ITS MASS EVACUATION PLANS AND DRILLS TOOK ON
FRESH URGENCY.

New England mobilized 1,287 local OCD councils overnight,
while the 168-year-old Massachusetts Committee on Public Safety
organized a home guard. Manuals on guerilla warfare circulated
among men whose civilian occupations had not prepared them for
the lethal karate chop or arming a grenade. Every community was
schematized down to the block level, where air raid wardens assumed responsibility for keeping all lights turned off during the
nightly blackouts. Air raid wardens wore white helmets and arm-
bands and carried tin whistles (sometimes from the five-and-ten
and stamped "Made in Japan"). House owners were encouraged to
place sand buckets and pails of water under attic roofs, and now
and then sirens or bells broke up town meetings and church socials.

OCD developed the Civil Air Patrol, composed of forty thousand part-time volunteers serving without pay and flying their own planes. They flew out of New England and East Coast airbases searching for Nazi subs (they spotted 173 probables) and guarding isolated beaches. So successful was CAP that the Army snatched it away in 1943.

OCD had always been a top-heavy bureaucracy, and under LaGuardia's successor, Harvard Law School dean James M. Landis, it stumbled into federal oblivion. The threatened air raids never materialized, and Landis achieved a dubious fame for his description of a blackout: "Such obscuration may be obtained by the termination of the illumination," or as the President tartly remarked, "Turn out the lights." But at the start of the war, no agency of government was more vital than Civil Defense.

Home front employees of the Rayon Corporation trained in first-aid procedures gather for a group photograph. (Hartford Collection, Hartford Public Library)

Barre, Vermont, employees of the New England Telephone and Telegraph company learned first aid techniques by practicing on each other. *(Houston Photograph Collection, Vermont State Archives)*

The logo for the Citizens Service Corps, a branch of Civilian Defense. *(Worcester Historical Museum)*

THE CITIZENS SERVICE CORPS
An Organization of Volunteers on the Home Front

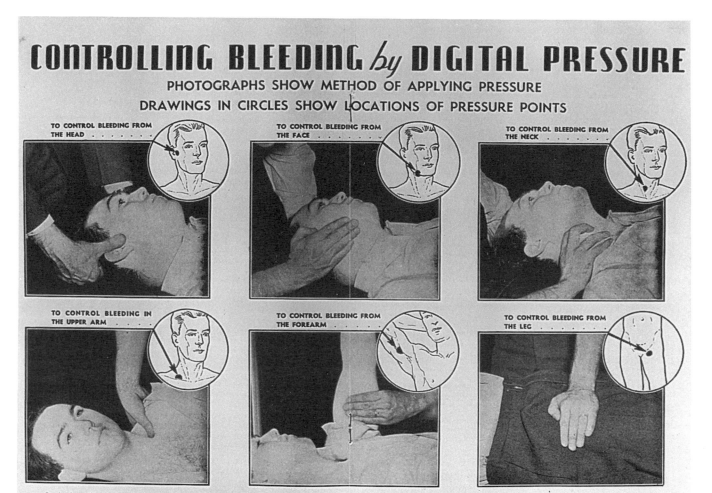

CONTROLLING BLEEDING *by* DIGITAL PRESSURE
PHOTOGRAPHS SHOW METHOD OF APPLYING PRESSURE
DRAWINGS IN CIRCLES SHOW LOCATIONS OF PRESSURE POINTS

TO CONTROL BLEEDING FROM THE HEAD . . . . . .

TO CONTROL BLEEDING FROM THE FACE . . . . . .

TO CONTROL BLEEDING FROM THE NECK . . . . . .

TO CONTROL BLEEDING IN THE UPPER ARM . . . . . .

TO CONTROL BLEEDING FROM THE FOREARM . . . . . .

TO CONTROL BLEEDING FROM THE LEG . . . . . .

Study these illustrations. Learn pressure points with a First Aider or your own doctor. Practise them at home. Master them BEFORE the emergency arises. If you possibly can arrange it, take the twenty hour First Aid Course as offered by the American Red Cross. Such knowledge may help you save a life, in time of peace as well as in time of war. Do your part too in accident prevention, for every accident is a monkey wrench in the machinery of National Defense.

Everyone was encouraged to
become familiar with first aid,
and few homes lacked a
Red Cross card prominently posted.
(Lynn Historical Society)

Air raid wardens and a Red Cross
official confer on civil defense
problems in Pittsfield. *(Berkshire
Athenaeum)*

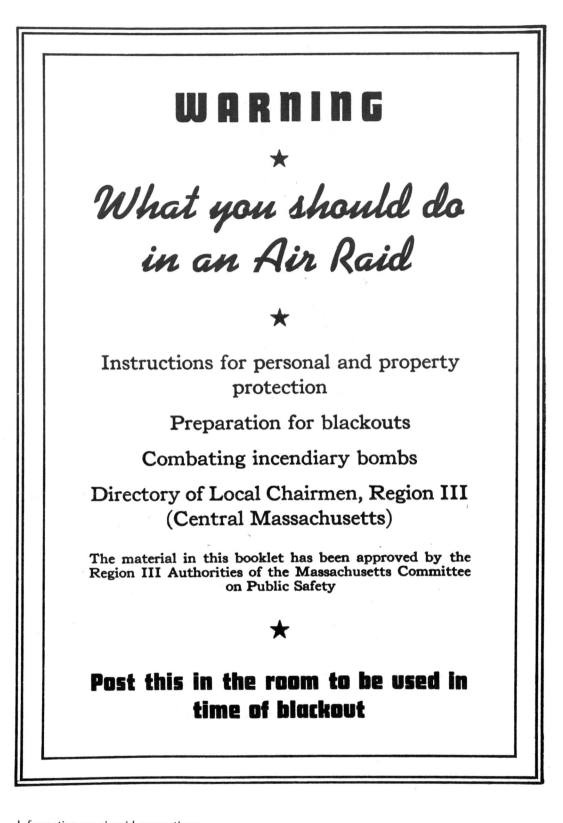

WARNING

★

What you should do in an Air Raid

★

Instructions for personal and property protection

Preparation for blackouts

Combating incendiary bombs

Directory of Local Chairmen, Region III (Central Massachusetts)

The material in this booklet has been approved by the Region III Authorities of the Massachusetts Committee on Public Safety

★

Post this in the room to be used in time of blackout

Information on air-raid precautions and blackout procedures was distributed to every household in New England. *(Worcester Historical Museum)*

★ WHAT TO DO IN AN AIR RAID ★

(a condensation of the official release, December 12, 1941 of the U. S. Office of Civilian Defense)

★ ★

1 – Keep Cool

Above all, keep cool. Don't lose your head.

Do not crowd streets, avoid chaos, prevent disorder and havoc.

You can fool the enemy. It is easy. If planes come over, stay where you are. Don't phone unnecessarily. The chance you will be hit is small. It is part of the risk we must take to win this war.

Until an alarm, go about your usual business and recreation in the ordinary way.

2 – Stay Home

The safest place in an air raid is at home.

If you are away from home, get under cover in the nearest shelter. Avoid crowded places. Stay off the streets.

The enemy wants you to run into the streets, create a mob, start a panic. DON'T DO IT!

Choose one member of the family to be the home air-raid warden— who will remember all the rules and what to do. Mother makes the best.

3 – Put Out Lights

Whether or not black-out is ordered, don't show more light than is necessary. If planes come over, put out or cover all lights at once— don't wait for the black-out order. The light that can't be seen will never guide a Jap. Remember a candle light may be seen for miles from the air.

Should you get an air-raid warning, remember to shut off gas stoves, gas furnaces, and gas pilot lights on both. Bomb explosions may blow them out from blast effect. Gas that collects may be explosive later.

4 – Lie Down

If bombs start to fall near you, lie down. You will feel the blast least that way, escape fragments or splinters.

The safest place is under a good stout table—the stronger the legs the better.

A mattress under a table combines comfort with safety.

The enemy may use explosive bombs or incendiary bombs, or both. If incendiaries are used, it's more important to deal with them than to be safe from blast. So defeat the incendiary with a SPRAY (never a splash or stream) of water, then go back to safety under a table in a refuge room.

5 – Stay Away From Windows

Glass shatters easily, so stay away from windows.

Don't go to windows and look out, in an air raid. It is a dangerous thing, and helps the enemy. The Air Raid Warden is out there watching for you. Again we say, get off the streets if planes come over.

At night, there is danger of being caught in blast from explosives.

Antiaircraft fire means falling shrapnel. You are safe from it indoors, away from windows. It's more important to shell a plane than it is to see it from a window.

N. B. — This pamphlet is not all inclusive. We hope it leads you to look up, read and study other available information on the subject. It was issued with all possible speed, with the knowledge that what it contained had been in demand months before war was declared.

Lynn Historical Society

THE MASSACHUSETTS COMMITTEE
ON PUBLIC SAFETY

HANDBOOK NO. 11

BLACKOUT INFORMATION *for* GENERAL PUBLIC

Issued by the

PROTECTION DIVISION

18 TREMONT ST.
BOSTON
January, 1942

Copyright by
THE MASSACHUSETTS COMMITTEE ON PUBLIC SAFETY
1942

50m-12-41-8122

OPAQUE SHADE SHIELDING LIGHT FROM WINDOW

WINDOW VENTILATOR

BLACK OUT CURTAINS READY TO BE PULLED TOGETHER FOR BLACKOUT PERIOD

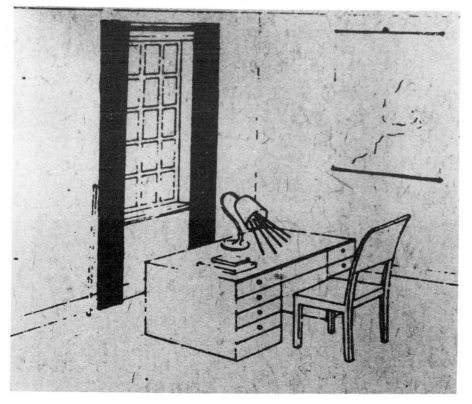

Every home was given directions for
blacking out windows and rooms.
(Worcester Historical Museum)

Neighborhood groups met regularly with group leaders. This was an important channel of civilian war information. *(Northeast Archives of Folklore and Oral History)*

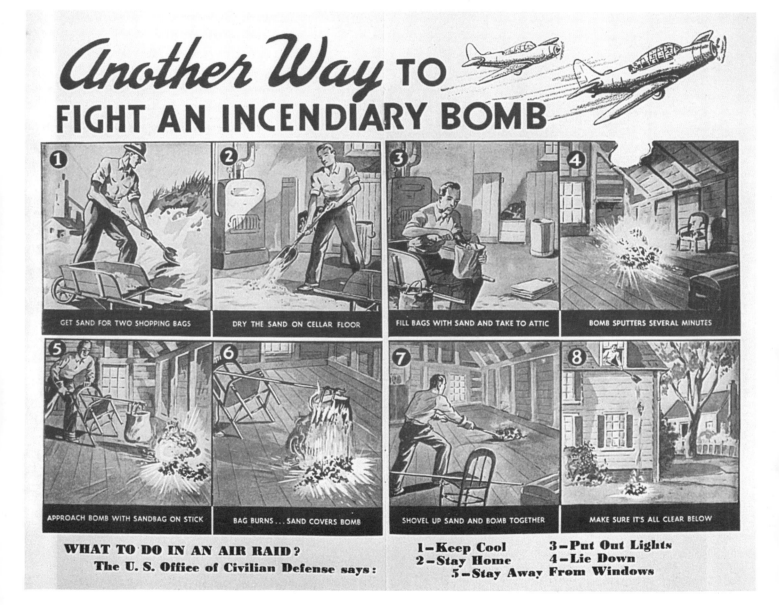

Another Way TO FIGHT AN INCENDIARY BOMB

1 — GET SAND FOR TWO SHOPPING BAGS

2 — DRY THE SAND ON CELLAR FLOOR

3 — FILL BAGS WITH SAND AND TAKE TO ATTIC

4 — BOMB SPUTTERS SEVERAL MINUTES

5 — APPROACH BOMB WITH SANDBAG ON STICK

6 — BAG BURNS... SAND COVERS BOMB

7 — SHOVEL UP SAND AND BOMB TOGETHER

8 — MAKE SURE IT'S ALL CLEAR BELOW

WHAT TO DO IN AN AIR RAID?
The U. S. Office of Civilian Defense says:

1 — Keep Cool   3 — Put Out Lights
2 — Stay Home   4 — Lie Down
    5 — Stay Away From Windows

Attics often had first aid instructions
posted as well as a bucket or
shopping bag full of sand in case
of incendiary bombing.
(Lynn Historical Society)

Protection Against Incendiary Bombs

by William M. Pierce
Supervising Chemical Engineer of THE EMPLOYERS' GROUP

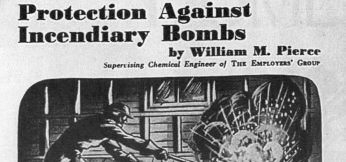

"shovel the bomb into the bucket of sand, then cover with sand."

IN peace time it is rather unusual that a destructive fire is started with deliberate intent. In 1939, there were approximately 655,000 fires in the United States and only 7,000 of these were of suspicious incendiary origin. This means that there were 648,000 fires occurring in spite of all the precautions taken to prevent them from either starting or spreading. The losses from these fires amounted to $270,000,000, even though the Fire Departments worked under the ideal conditions to keep these losses down.

Imagine, if you can, the amount of loss which would result from a series of air raids where the main weapon was incendiary bombs. Each bomber can carry 2,000 small magnesium incendiary bombs, and it has been estimated that 75 bombs out of the 2,000 will start serious fires. If each raid consists of 100 bombers, there will be 7,500 serious fires started as a result of each raid. The fires would be concentrated along a line of about three miles with a fire every 60 yards. The regular Fire Department would only be able to deal with a comparatively small number of these fires because under ordinary conditions they know there will only be a very small number of fires occurring at any one time. In addition the roads may be impassable and the water supply may be considerably decreased. Also, the type of fire which has been caused is different from that ordinarily encountered. A stream of water played on incendiary bombs will only increase the intensity of the fire. This is not a particularly pleasant picture, but we believe this emphasizes the necessity of everyone being prepared for just such an emergency and knowing what to do.

Because of the seriousness of the situation and the peculiar nature of incendiary bombs, a short des-

[2]

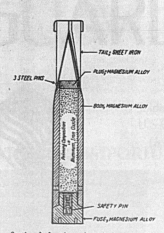

Sectional drawing of typical magnesium incendiary bomb

cription of their composition and properties is desirable. The most efficient type which might be encountered is the Electron Bomb, which weighs about two pounds and consists of a thick walled magnesium cylinder filled with thermite. The thermite is ignited by a percussion cap in the nose of the bomb which in turn ignites the magnesium, which is the actual incendiary agent. Once this bomb has been ignited it will burn from 10-15 minutes at temperatures of about 2,000 degrees Fahrenheit. The chief value of this type of bomb as an incendiary agent is that it reacts violently with water, causing more intense fire rather than putting it out. The proper method of extinguishing these bombs depends on the time they are located and also whether or not there is any considerable fire surrounding the bomb. If the bomb can be reached within two minutes of the time it lands, it may be possible to smother it, using sand. The details of the sand

method of handling are as follows:

If possible, the man should be protected with a fire-fighting mask or gas-tight goggles and heavy gloves. A wet blanket should be used to protect the man's back from burning fragments. Half a bucket of sand is placed on the floor as near the bomb as possible. With a long handled shovel or pusher, the operator places sand around and on top of the bomb. It is then possible to shovel the bomb into the bucket on top of the remaining sand, and then cover the bomb with sand from the floor. The bucket is then removed from the building to a safe place, using the handle of the shovel to transport the bucket.

Generally, the bomb will have set fire to a considerable amount of surrounding material, so water must be used. In handling bombs by this method, two persons are required. One man is necessary to operate the hose and a second to operate the pump. It is possible a third man can be used to replenish the water in the bucket and to relieve the pump operator. The details are as follows: One man, wearing any protective equipment, such as gloves, mask or goggles, which may be available, approaches the bomb to a distance where the stream can easily be directed. He first extinguishes any fire which may have been started by the bomb, playing a stream of water directly upon this fire. A stirrup pump, a soda-acid fire extinguisher, water from an ordinary garden hose providing the water pressure is sufficient, or an Indian pump could be used. As soon as this fire has been put out a spray is used on the bomb itself until it is burned out. The purpose of the spray is to hasten the ignition of the bomb to get rid of it. It is generally necessary to use about

[3]

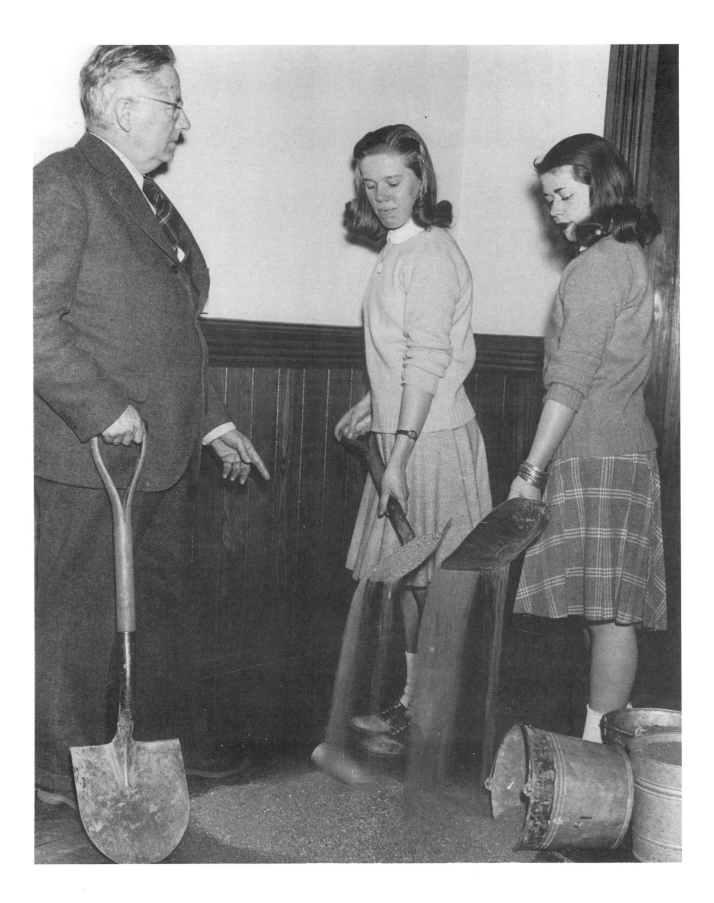

Wilson T. Moog, who was a professor of music, demonstrates fire-fighting techniques against incendiary bombs to Smith College students. *(Smith College Archives)*

A fire extinguisher and a shield against incendiary bombs became a part of Smith College dormitory life. *(Smith College Archives)*

Cartoonist Milton Caniff ("Terry and the Pirates") illustrated scores of civil defense pamphlets. Using the techniques of movies, close-ups, dramatic camera angles, and lighting, Caniff portrayed dauntless Americans determined to see the job through. *(Worcester Historical Museum)*

The Yacht Patrol, shown here patroling the coast of Maine. Yachts and fishing boats were converted to patrol boats to guard the coast from German submarines and aircraft. *(Photo courtesy Aubrey Young, Camden, Maine)*

The New England coast bristled with lookout posts such as this one commanding an ocean view at Cape Porpoise, Maine. *(Kennebunkport Historical Society)*

VICTORY

A trio of Portland youngsters
hail the red, white and blue.
(The Portland Press Herald)

O N AUGUST 14, 1945, A CLOUDY TUESDAY AFTERNOON, READERS OF *THE BOSTON EVENING GLOBE* RED STREAK FINAL (THIRTY-SIX PAGES, THREE CENTS) SAW A FRONT PAGE FILLED BY TIERS OF HEADLINES: *"OFFICIAL / PRESIDENT TRUMAN ANNOUNCES/ JAPS SURRENDER / THIS MEANS END OF WAR / V-J DAY COMING LATER / MACARTHUR TO ACCEPT TERMS."*

The terse Associated Press bulletin read in its entirety: "President Truman announced at 7:00 P.M. EWT tonight Japanese acceptance of surrender terms. They will be accepted by General Douglas MacArthur when arrangements can be completed."

The word "Official" was necessary because of the false alarm triggered by the United Press at 9:30 P.M. on August 12. The bogus surrender announcement touched off premature celebrations that, notwithstanding the UP's quashing of the bulletin ten minutes later, continued well into the night. A cheering throng in Worcester ignited a downtown bonfire that firemen were powerless to control. Northern Maine and Vermont heard a prerecorded radio peace message from Canadian Prime Minister MacKenzie King. Firecrackers sputtered across Boston's Chinatown. The emotional tensions released on August 14 and on V-J Day, August 15 (despite President Truman's announcement that V-J Day would be delayed until the actual signing of peace documents), spilled over like lava from a pent-up volcano.

During the first months of 1945 the war had telescoped into its most momentous phase. April alone saw the death of three leaders who symbolized an epoch of world history: Mussolini, Roosevelt, and Hitler. V-E Day was May 8, but Boston and New England, though relieved by the news of the end of the war in Europe, largely shunned revelry. There was stubborn resistance on Okinawa still, and shipyards and aircraft factories remained in operation around the clock. Then, on August 6, the first atomic bomb exploded over Hiroshima. In the radiation labs of Harvard and M.I.T., scientists understood what this signified, but ordinary New Englanders had for the most part never heard of nuclear energy. Roy Hoopes records the experience of Cathleen Schurr, who, earlier in the war, had been on a ship torpedoed in the Atlantic:

"On V-J Day we were on holiday at Orleans on Cape Cod. We didn't have a radio, but somebody had one on in a car, and I remember going out and sitting on the ground alongside the car and hearing the news. We all looked at each other and said something about church and went to a service in a little traditional New England white chapel. It was a tiny place that probably didn't hold more than forty to fifty people, beautifully white. It was run by an elderly gentleman and his wife, who kept goats and made bracelets. I remember that during the so-called minister's belabored sermon celebrating the end of this awful holocaust, he couldn't remember the word for the bomb. He stumbled over it, and the wife, who obviously was the intelligence of the family, called out

Throngs gathered everywhere
to celebrate peace. Here is the
World War II Victory Parade
in Keene, New Hampshire.
*(Historical Society of
Cheshire County)*

Victory Night on Tremont Street,
Boston, and the euphoria of
the war's sudden ending.
(The Christian Science Monitor)

Sailors in Boston's Chinatown celebrate Japan's surrender. The newsboy hawking papers on the street would vanish in the postwar years. *(The Christian Science Monitor)*

from the back of the chapel, 'Atom bomb.' I can't remember that he said anything important; we were all so relieved and so happy. It seemed to me that his attitude was that the atom bomb had 'saved us'—that this is what it took to end this terrible war."

Although thoughtful people marked the onset of peace with meditation, thanksgiving, and religious observance, a wave of antic exhilaration swept New England. It was a revival of Armistice Night in 1918—New Year's Eve magnified. Honking motor cavalcades inched along the streets of every New England city. Church bells rang. Crowds swirled, blowing horns and brandishing noisemakers. "There was no noteworthy disorder," *The Christian Science Monitor* observed, "but the city had the wildest celebration it has ever seen." Smaller communities celebrated in more decorous fashion: The victory parade organized in Keene, New Hampshire, expressed the patriotic sentiment of the war years in a cavalcade of flags and marching bands. To be sure, the festivities did not lack ugly incidents. Disturbances broke out in New Bedford; during an impromptu parade through the business district policemen tried to take a fractious sailor into custody. His friends intervened, and the ensuing mêleé escalated into a full-blown riot in which state guardsmen with fixed bayonets reinforced naval police. Nine arrests resulted.

Incidents of violence were rare, however; on the whole, the revelers, though boisterous, were good-humored, and it should be noted that not everyone's idea of bliss consisted of joining a raucous crowd. On August 15 gasoline rationing ended, and much of New England simply tanked up for the first ration-free auto ride since Pearl Harbor. Not since the twenties had a jaunt in the family car assumed such importance. And perhaps the other overlooked aspect of V-J night is the fact that it ushered in a new era of electronic communication. The largest audience in broadcasting history — more radio listeners than there were for Pearl Harbor or the funeral rites of Franklin D. Roosevelt — heard the sirens and bells of V-J night, for the preceding days had been a roller-coaster of conflicting bulletins about Washington's negotiations with Japan. You had to tune in to stay abreast of events. The communications industry now considered itself an essential adjunct of government. In January 1945, the Columbia Broadcasting System advertised that over the past three years of war, "CBS used a total of 8,686 hours . . . to tell the American people how the war was being won, how to help win it . . . 46,062 separate CBS broadcasts offered 56,667 distinct ideas forwarding the march to victory."

That night in New England it seemed Americans could at last realize their wartime ideals of safety from war and protection against Depression. The war was a turning point for women and to some degree for blacks, who in spite of white racism made the great migration to northern industry with mounting expectations. Veterans came home to a postwar society which on the surface resembled the New England they had left — Boston, for example, with its ethnic rivalries and James M. Curley still a political force, although jailed in Danbury, Connecticut, for mail fraud — but which in fact was a transformed world.

In 1945, fifteen million Americans were living in sites other than the place they had been on December 7, 1941. Between October 1945, and February 1946, three-quarters of a million men and women were separated from the armed forces on the basis of a point system involving seniority and length of service. By June 1946, the process of demobilization was virtually complete:

Hartford store front draped in
memoriam for President Franklin D.
Roosevelt, April 13, 1945.
(Tony DeBonee)

The headline Americans waited for.
The war in the Pacific, however,
still continued. *(Tony DeBonee)*

12,807,000 Americans had come back to civilian life. By June 30, 1947, living World War II veterans attained an average of 29.1 years old, according to the statistical records. World War II veterans and their immediate families comprised almost one-fourth of the total U.S. population. Three-fifths were married and two-thirds resided in suburban areas.

Returning to civilian life began for the veteran at a mustering-out center like the Fargo Building in South Boston or Fort Devens. His discharge papers would arrive in the mail along with, perhaps, a cordial letter of farewell signed by James Forrestal, Secretary of the Navy, urging reenlistment. Although the country had come through the war relatively unscathed and was flexing its economic muscle, there was immediate unemployment caused by the closing of the shipyards and defense plants. Many women and minorities felt the brunt of the old adage, "last hired, first fired." Reconversion had begun; one of its effects was to pit white ethnic groups who had been on the bottom of the totem pole — Italians, Mexicans, Poles, Jews — against blacks and women who had assumed skilled jobs in industry.

The veteran seeking employment, however, usually began at the 52-20 club, the $20 weekly unemployment check until eligibility ran out at the end of a year. In Harvard Square a daily queue coiled in front of the Veterans Administration office, the men still wearing khakis or bomber jackets or dungarees from which all insignia had been razored. The 52-20 club often was just that: a refuge for those who found the transition to civilian life painful. They reunited every week in a drab, smokey room, waiting for their number to be called, chatting amidst the familiar comfortable tedium of a military bureaucracy like the lair of a quartermaster or a company clerk.

The GI Bill of Rights — more officially, the Serviceman's Readjustment Act — enacted by Congress in 1944, supplanted the 52-20 club with sweeping provisions: among them, full tuition and supplementary allowances to support veterans enrolled in educational programs on any level. Furthermore, the Veterans Administration would guarantee half the amount of loans necessary for the establishment of small businesses, the purchase of farms, or the buying of a home on a thirty-year mortgage. The bill constituted a social revolution backed, ironically, by the American Legion, a potent political force noted for its conservatism.

Then as now a leading New England industry, education began a postwar expansion. The implications of the GI Bill were felt in every school, college, and university. Before the war a college education was somewhat elitist; afterward, it became as common and necessary as a high-school diploma. Students whose parents aspired to a college degree, but were blocked by financial circumstances, lived out the parental dream. The new democracy of higher education took in undergraduates in their mid-twenties or even older who challenged many of the assumptions of professors and administrators. On every campus, from Harvard's, where the veterans lived near Memorial Drive, to Brown University, where they were scattered around College Hill, housing became an issue. One of the most familiar sights of the immediate postwar period in New England was the cluster of Quonset huts or other provisional housing for veterans and their families scrimping along under the GI Bill.

The shortage of housing prompted satire on the Levittowns and

To those who were in it, the war seemed endless, but Victory Parades like Keene, New Hampshire's, on August 14, 1945, signalled that peace had come at last to the home front. *(Historical Society of Cheshire County)*

similar developments where prefab structures surrendered to utility. But veterans who were cramped in trailers, from which they commuted to the University of Vermont and Wesleyan, were buoyed by future expectations denied to most during the Depression years. Anyone who had made a steady wage then did not change jobs. However, the veteran in postwar New England was, above all, upward mobile, willing to endure temporary deprivation for long-term awards. Out of the war came both the end of a way of life and the rise of a new middle class eager to savor prosperity. Their affluence promised more consumer goods, and within a few years shopping malls would encroach upon fields and woodlands.

The veteran was a political power, and politicians such as John F. Kennedy, Richard Nixon, and Joseph McCarthy, who had served in the armed forces, prepared to use that power. Making his run for Congress in the fall of 1946, Kennedy assembled a team of veterans: "Red" Fay, his fellow naval officer; Torbert MacDonald; Mark Dalton, a newspaperman and lawyer then in the 52-20 club; and his brother Robert Kennedy, a Navy enlisted man. Politically, the country had embarked on an internationalism in marked contrast to the isolationist years before the war when few politicians felt obliged to dabble in foreign affairs. The veteran could remember a time when America, sheltered by two oceans, felt protected from the ancient disputes and ancestral quarrels of Europe and Asia. Yet the United States participated in the occupation of Berlin and Japan. Before most veterans left the service, Churchill had delivered his Iron Curtain speech, Stalin was clearly as menacing as Hitler had been, and planners in Washington were preaching a defense policy that would encircle the Soviet Union with American bases for strategic bombers armed with atomic weapons.

The world the New England veteran saw in those first months was far from reassuring. He had marched off to war from a simpler country, where big government and big business and what Dwight Eisenhower was to call "the military-industrial complex" did not influence the nation's world view. He had returned to a different culture of higher taxes, permanent inflation, and an economy geared to global engines. There was more big business in government; there was less local autonomy. Could he be blamed for a certain apprehension, as if the bells of victory were tolling for the past?